W9-CUP-080

What others are saying about this book:

"This is a wonderful book full of practical advice which will contribute to further self-understanding and higher consciousness. Marilyn is a marvelous human being and outstanding hypnotherapist who has helped me with my personal growth and positive changes in my life. She brings a wealth of experience and practical know-how into this extremely readable and remarkable book. You will be a better person for reading it!"

> J. Gary Gwilliam
> President, California Trial Lawyers Association,
> 1988

"This is one of the most valuable guides I have read toward the discovery of the authentic self. It goes beyond personality, beyond patching up the wounded persona, to the core or essence of the Self."

> Dennis Michael Harness
> PhD in Counseling Psychology

"This is a wonderful, wonderful book. It's rational, sane, presented in a most professional way. Even the most skeptical people will accept this. It's wonderful. I want to buy six copies for people I know."

> Maxine Ashcraft
> Regional Marketing Director,
> Lenfest Communications

"The key to the deepest level of healing is remembering and experiencing who you really are in every cell on every level of your being. Marilyn Gordon's book has revealed this essential truth in a profound way."

> Gabriel Cousens, MD
> Holistic Physician, Director of Tree of Life
> Seminars, author of SPIRITUAL NUTRITION
> AND THE RAINBOW DIET and
> SEVEN-FOLD PEACE

"Marilyn is a compassionate and skilled hypnotherapist whose gift for touching people's lives comes through beautifully in her book. She presents very practical and moving ways to cut through the emotional pain and achieve more of your human potential."

Bob Oliver, Certified Hypnotherapist

"I found myself entranced. I read the whole thing through without stopping. Usually self-help or hypnosis books tend to be either dry or condescending; yours is neither. Also you don't try to force one belief or religion on your readers. This is truly a book for everyone. Reading your book is a form of healing, like talking with a wise friend. I was left with a sense of peace and well-being. I want to give copies to all my friends."

Kathy Thornton

"It's wonderful; it has touched me. I could feel the presence of a healing power as I was reading it."

Carla Radosta

"I fell in love with it. It's clear, informational, laid out in an organized way. The stories aren't just about isolated people with problems—but universal issues. It's uplifting and readable with a lot of profound insight. Terrific."

Nora Cousens, RPT

"It's a beautiful book."

Shree Pickar

*For Richard —
With love,
Marilyn Gordon
4-91*

Healing is Remembering Who You Are

*A Guide for Healing Your Mind,
Your Emotions, and Your Life*

Marilyn Gordon
Certified Hypnotherapist

Foreword by Ormand McGill,
"Dean of American Hypnotists"

WISE WORD Publishing

Copyright ©1991 by Marilyn Gordon

WiseWord Publishing
PO Box 10795
Oakland, CA 94610
(415) 547-8823

Library of Congress Catalog Card Number 90-71400
ISBN 0-9627762-0-3

All rights reserved. No part of this book may be
reproduced or transmitted in any form by any means,
electronic or mechanical, including photocopying,
recording, or by any information storage and retrieval-
system, without permission in writing from the
author, except for the inclusion of brief quotations in
a review.

Cover and book design: Carla Radosta
Cover illustration: Pablo Haz
Photography: Claudia Marseille

First edition 1991
Printed in the United States
10 9 8 7 6 5 4 3 2 1

Dedicated to all of us
on the great path of healing.

Contents

Thanks to all who made their contributions to this book...

....to those whose healing stories are told here

....to those who helped with this project, especially Keith Campbell, David Kenneth Waldman, Carla Radosta, Barbara Campbell, Tobey Kaplan, and Jean Sibley

....to my mother and my daughter, with love

....to my inner guide, SamuEl, for helping the wisdom to flow and for constant encouragement

....to great teachers: Baba, Werner, Ormand, and others

....to those who've helped me in wonderful ways, including Bob Oliver, Jimmy Hernandez, Joe Masri, Gary Gwilliam, Nora and Gabriel Cousens, Kay Heatherly, Dennis Michael Harness, Eve Crain, Carolyn Silas-Sams, John d'Ambrogio, Cathy Valdez, Charlie Briggs, Carol Nyhoff, The Hoosin Family, Shree Pickar, Irene Sazer and David Adee, Frances Hailman, Lee Bresloff, Hugh McLoone, Pablo Haz, Max Ashcraft, Cynthia Greenberg, Kathy Thornton, Karen Hogan, Debby and Jimmy Stack, Maggie Romero, Duane Hall, Anne Langford, Anne Ponder, Nina and Lisa Kindblad and Ken Burke, Rose, Jordan Rothstein, Maureen Longworth, Maria Tubbs, Bill Failing, Jesse Arcenaux, Barbara Kaplan, Steve Brown, and others. And to all of you I haven't mentioned, I thank you, too.

....to my extraordinary clients who inspire me with their healing powers and fascinating lives

....to my grandmother who gave me so much love

....to my essence where I find my peace.

Foreword

You hold in your hands a unique book. It is a book on hypnotherapy presented in a poetic way. Its author, Marilyn Gordon, is a certified hypnotherapist with the American Council of Hypnotist Examiners. Her popular audio tapes called "WonderWords" have won wide acclaim. In her hypnotherapy practice, she works with practical matters, such as helping people to lose weight, stop smoking, handle stress, develop self-confidence—all the significant things that hypnotherapists do. But in this book, and in her practice as well, she takes you beyond the conventional, literally into the realm of metaphysics (meaning "beyond the physical") and plumbs the depths of your inner being in a way remindful of Gibran.

HEALING IS REMEMBERING WHO YOU ARE is a very personal book both for its author and its reader. Marilyn Gordon speaks freely of her own conflicts with life, her studies of yoga, meditation, and ways through which she found inner peace, healing of her fears and conflicts, and how she created for herself a healthful life. She shares what she has found helpful to herself, giving you both the ways and the means for reaching through to your ESSENCE of being.

Marilyn Gordon writes of timeless truths in a way that makes the reader feel he or she is taking a walk in a quiet woods, or bathing in a cool stream; it soothes the troubled soul and heals the spirit.

HEALING IS REMEMBERING WHO YOU ARE is a self-help book that is to be read, studied, and used not only with an open mind but with an open heart as well. It is for everyone.

Ormand McGill
Palo Alto, CA   1990

[Ormand McGill is called the "Dean of American Hypnotists". He is the author of sixteen books over the past half century, including many classics. He is a gentle, loving hypnotist, teacher, author, and wise being.]

"When one allows oneself quietly
to experience the hurtful wound and the
memories connected with it, the golden elixir will flow
out of it, healing it, and filling the emptiness
with the beautiful sweet fullness that will melt the heart,
erase the mind, and bring about contentment that
the individual has been thirsting for."

A.H.Almaas

Your
Healing
Essence

In 1970, someone suggested I go to a yoga class. I needed something. I was a burnt-out, frazzled ex-teacher, and I desperately needed to find some peace. I went to a building that smelled of fresh-baked bread, incense, and sweet wood, and I climbed the stairs to an upper room full of spacious windows and green vibrant plants. We did yoga postures, and then we did something that changed my life forever; we relaxed so deeply, that I was transported into another state of consciousness. I had never been able to relax this way before. It soothed my raw nerves, but it also did much more. It altered my vision, my perspective. It pointed me inward to my own essence. And from that point on, I dedicated myself to understanding what that essence was about.

Essence is a strong inner core.

I came to learn that this essence is a strong inner core that belongs to everyone; it has the qualities of love, wisdom, and strength. I realized that it's a natural state of elevated consciousness, a natural high of love and power that everyone is looking for and is most often trying to find in outward ways—looking for the sweetness of love in sweet food—or for the closeness in relationship—or for the re-experience of that original state in drugs or alcohol. I found that the loss of this state is experienced as loneliness, abandonment, depression and lack of love. Underneath all the problems of life, underneath the anger, illness, grief, or feelings of unworthiness, there is an essence that can heal.

The child knows essence naturally.

Babies have the natural experience of this essence. Later our natural illumination is dimmed as we learn from parents and others that our personality is all that exists. For the rest of our lives we're looking to get back to that original state of love. Most adult problems stem from lack of contact with the inner experience of essence, but fortunately we do have the fundamental capacity for healing.

Barriers to essence can be dissolved.

Healing pain, stress, fear and abuse is not about seeking external solutions or palliatives. It is about remembering this deep inner core that has been covered over by layer upon layer of worldly experience, conditioning, and personality. While therapy is often about examining the issues of the personality, inner healing or "essence hypnotherapy" or "remembering" is about going directly to the place of love and understanding and from this place dissolving the barriers that are in the way of self-knowledge. It is about peeling off the layers of life experiences and revealing your essence to yourself once again.

Shine the light of essence to heal old wounds.

When you free this essence, then other parts of you—weaker, disenfranchised parts of your personality—are seen in a new way. When you shine a light on these places, the illumination changes them. Sometimes the light disintegrates the weaker parts, and they disappear—but more often, it makes them whole. By shedding light on the difficult places in your personality, you can bring to them love, wisdom, peace, joy, and understanding—and they will never again be the same. The process is not "therapy"— but a return to who you really are.

Healing is the work of a lifetime.

When you make contact with your essence and you have experiences of healing, you're not "healed" in a final sense. Healing is the work of a lifetime, and you usually find that you have several main issues that keep cycling back into your life, often at different levels each time they return. So you might heal a fear, and then it might reappear at another time in your life if you have some more learning to do. Healing does not always mean that the issue is gone. It means that you're able to be more objective about your situation and more aware of your inner resources for healing it.

You can get in touch with your essence.

Experiencing your essence often involves going within, through hypnosis, meditation, or other methods that focus you inward. But essence can also be experienced while you're in motion, at any time or any place. You may have experienced it when your mind stopped chattering for that ecstatic moment and you feel uplifted, in a kind of flow. You may have been playing a musical instrument, and the music comes through you as if you're simply an instrument yourself through which the music passes. Or you're running, and you feel an exhilaration, as if your body and you and the earth were all one energy. Or you're making love, and you feel lifted up beyond ordinary reality.

To experience essence, it helps to have a regular practice of one form or another, of meditation or yoga or chanting or hypnosis or creative expression or love. In another chapter, you will find the script for a tape that you can make for yourself that will help you to have this experience. This book is about letting your experience of essence heal all other parts of yourself, especially your fears, anger, grief, weaknesses, challenges, and all parts of yourself that are in need of support and love.

As you read on, you will find stories about particular issues of healing. Each story is a composite of actual hypnotherapy experiences. You will be able to understand what hypnotherapy is, how it's done, and how your own essence can heal your wounds. Remember as you read, that because healing is the work of an entire lifetime, each story is only a chapter in each person's journey.

I hope that you will find reflections of yourself on these pages and that reading this book inspires healing experiences of your own.

"…what you are striving to become in actuality is what you already are in essence."

Ralph Blum

Journey to Self-Knowledge:

The Path to Your Essence

On the path to your healing essence, many questions may arise, such as, "Why do I need healing? What is my purpose for being in this world? Why do we have to suffer? How can I be happy?" Here are a few ways of looking at these profound issues.

Coming to Terms with Suffering

Even though there is great joy and beauty everywhere, there is also great suffering and pain. You see families without homes, children born with drug defects, starving mothers and their babies, senseless taking of lives. Sometimes it's hard not to just sit and weep for humanity. And yet, when you take a step back and look at the larger picture, you begin to understand that each human being is learning some type of lesson. Some of these lessons are extremely tough; others are much easier to bear. Whatever may be the degree of suffering, something is being accomplished by the suffering. Someone may be undergoing some type of purification; perhaps someone is learning how to be strong, how to have fortitude in the face of great obstacles.

Someone may be learning what it is like to lose a child or a mate; another is learning how to live on the streets; another is given the lessons inherent in a terminal or debilitating illness; and yet another is learning about violence. And for those who have been given difficult lessons, these challenges are what you may need for your growth. Those who have impairments of the physical body, family difficulties, financial challenges you may be learning something important from your circumstance. Are you learning compassion for others? Are you learning strength or fortitude or the acceptance of your situation? Are you learning how to love through this situation? Are you learning how to have inner peace no matter what appears on the outer? The answer to your own particular situation will come through you when you are able to listen to its message. It may be difficult to find through your pain or your loss, but it is there. And you will find that there is a perfection to everything, a greater plan for your personal evolution that may not make sense on the physical level, but that has a meaning beyond mere appearances.

Suffering does its work on you and can open you in many ways. It can embitter you, or it can open you if you let it. It can transform you. If you feel hurt or separate or alone, resources often come from within you to make you into someone who is deepened by your experience. Crying, for example, does wash the windows of the soul. Deep feelings can come forth like a volcano's molten hot lava which, when cooled, becomes the most purified form of ash.

Suffering is given to you as a challenge, a prod to growth, a tool to help you evolve. A great deal of suffering occurs because we are attached to things always being the same as they were before. The sadness of this is that it is the nature of the physical universe to change incessantly. What remains constant on this earth? Loved ones are taken away or go away or never loved us or loved us the wrong way. Some of these experiences are very painful, and yet it is through this pain that you can be moved to your next level of growth. Through this suffering, you can reach inside yourself and find your greatest qualities of strength, personal power, love, independent action, perseverance, and depth. The experience of love and suffering is a catalyst for true transformation because it reaches deep inside of you almost as if it were a hand reaching into your heart and pulling you out of your present state and into your next.

The more resilient you are, the more you can handle the fluctuations of life. Not only do you survive the trials, but you become greater because of them. It is a fire which burns you through and through, and out of the ashes, you are born into new life.

The wise beings of all time tell us also that the ups and downs of our lives are like plays or dramas, unreal illusions, that push us to find some greater truth. This is why so many look within to find that which does not change, that which is a solid inner core of love, peace, deep comfort, and true joy.

Dealing with Pain

Whether your pain is physical or emotional, it can be an instructive and deepening force, a true vehicle for self-knowledge. Pain can teach you so much. If you allow it to move through you without blocking it, it can serve to cleanse you. If you cry and yell, grieve and mourn, shed tears, clear your vocal chords and your throat, allow life energy to course through all of your muscles, you can free yourself from blockages. Pain can serve to teach you about the suffering of all beings on this planet; it can soften you to the common bond of humanity that links us together. Pain can be a tool to help you break through the barriers of your personality, to go deeper than the persona or image that you present to the everyday world.

Someone once said that your pain is just the breaking of the shell that encloses your understanding. Another speaks of pain with an even more graphic metaphor: it is God tearing our flesh in shreds and spilling our blood in streams to remind us of our oneness with the One by lifting off the veils of illusion that normally keep us blind.

Most people want to anesthetize their pain; this is

why so many take substances into their bodies, looking for comfort, for numbness, for that altered consciousness in which pain does not exist.

But your pain has much to teach you. Is your pain asking you to listen to the underlying message, to pay attention to the problem at hand—not to simply alleviate the symptom? Can your pain be telling you to love more fully, to find a way to experience more harmony with yourself and with others and with the universe? You can listen to your distress and open to it. The more you allow it, the more it can teach you and then take its leave.

Some people can transcend pain. If you have explored it fully, it may be possible to leap into another consciousness state where you are freed from the pain entirely. Some people who have been tortured, for example, who have been in great agony, have been able to find a state of reverie, where they can rest their minds and transcend their pain. One man was on an operating table, and he began to hemorrhage profusely. There was no time for him to receive more anesthesia, and the pain was excruciating. His mind went to a sun-filled beach he had known as a child, and he played there while the surgeons completed the operation. For him it was a painless, distant dream.

Emotional pain can also be very instructive. Because it can grab you in your most vulnerable places, at your insecurities, your inner core, it can be an avenue to getting to places that are deep inside of you. Without this, you might live on more superficial and uncaring levels. Emotional pain can deepen you; if you don't harden around it, it can open secret places inside of you. Through your own pain, you can unite with others who are experiencing theirs as well. You can unite with captives, hostages, and fellow beings everywhere. You open to them. And in their suffering, they too are being opened. And all of you can open to the unity of human hearts. Pain can have an evolutionary quality; it can serve to bring you forward step by step on your evolutionary path. It can enhance and educate you.

Caring for Others' Suffering

You can develop more and more compassion, and it can bring you out of your own anger, resentment, hatred, and fear. Developing compassion requires an opening of your heart—seeing with the eyes of love—and noticing that everyone is suffering in one way or another. Some people don't seem to be suffering at all; their lives seem charmed. But if you stand back and look at the larger picture, you come into the wisdom that everyone is suffering—if only the suffering of being locked in a human body with the possibility of disease and death that the body presents. Everyone suffers loss; everyone suffers leavings and goodbyes, some of them temporary, and some of them permanent. Everyone suffers the pain of the physical body and illness. Caring for the suffering of others can uplift you. In one respect, it can take your mind off your own suffering, and it can also unite you with the entire body of human life. We are all in this together. It is always uplifting to help to alleviate the suffering of others, to bring comfort, to spread your love around, to experience being peaceful in the midst of chaos, to aid and assist wherever needed. If you feel desperate or alone, opening your heart to compassion can help you overcome these feelings and can give your life purpose.

It is also important to have compassion for yourself, especially if you are one of those who is hard on yourself. If you have a problem and you have been working on it for a long time, it is possible to reduce your self-condemnation. Embrace your own self, open your heart to your own self, and give yourself love. Then that compassion can expand and touch the whole of humanity, beginning with you.

Taking Responsibility

When you were a child, you were heavily programmed by the people in your life. You may have been told, for example, that you wouldn't amount to anything or that you were stupid or that you didn't have what it takes to make it in this world. But now you are no longer this child, and ultimately you have to take responsibility for buying whatever negative garbage was thrown your way. Now you have the opportunity to tell your own self that these judgments are simply not so, and that any current negativity you have is your own. This means that because you accept responsibility for buying it, you can now disown it, let it go, and come into greater truth about your identity and your own real worth. So a thought or feeling of unworthiness may come up, and you can now say to yourself, "No, that is not at all true. I am a great human being, and within me is love."—and you can remember who you are. This opportunity is given to you at any moment of any day, and you can do it through your own healing power.

Understanding Karma and Destiny

Many great beings believe that we have numerous lifetimes and that we are working on issues and relationships that go back before this one. Sometimes you may feel that no matter how many affirmations you do or how much therapy you have, you still judge yourself a lot, or you don't seem to make ends meet financially, or you still have that sticky relationship. Karmic understanding of this is that your life includes the lessons you've either brought here from the past or that you agreed to work through before you came here; your karma is your "destiny".

The good news is that you may be on the verge of winding up that karma. Taking responsibility for it, doing whatever you can to be as conscious about it as possible, and remembering who you really are, these are steps toward completing whatever you may have come here to complete.

Finding the Meaning of Healing

It means that you are able to find a level of awareness in which there is peace or harmony, and this eventually transforms your external reality. You are able to go deeply enough inside to find a core of truth. When you experience it, you feel equanimity or peace. This is why healing is remembering who you are. You find this core of strength, peace, and love within yourself, your true nature, and from this place, you uplift and transform the other parts of yourself that have forgotten the truth.

Most of the time, you don't experience healing all at once; you heal in layers, in increments, in doses; and as I say over and over again in this book, healing is the work of a lifetime. You go through many doorways. Layer upon layer, you heal a thought, a pattern, an image, a pain, a fear, an old emotion, an old picture or habit, a relationship.

And what precipitates this healing more than anything else is your intention to heal, your willingness. Those who are in denial usually don't make these changes. Your intent to heal sets your will in motion, and also calls forth all the forces of healing in the universe. It is true that sometimes you need to not heal your situation, your challenge, right away. You need to let it be. Everything has its own perfect timing, and you can tune in and sense your readiness. Usually you know when you're ready if you sense that you've had absolutely enough of your situation, and you feel from deep within yourself the possiblity of change. This is a great healing opportunity.

Knowing the Basic Core of Love.

When you experience your basic core of love, you cease to feel alienated and separate. You mirror, or remember, that you are a part of the vibrating love of the universe. This is why love is a state of healing; by experiencing your essence, you reunite with the universal. Consider that all matter in the universe is vibrating and that the essence of this vibration is love and that this love is the fundamental ecstasy of the universe. Your experience of love expands you beyond your ordinary boundaries and lifts you into a healing consciousness.

Even though you're made of love, you don't always experience it. You feel alienated or hurt or angry or fearful—or you have physical symptoms such as pain or illness. So many hearts are hurting because of the need for love—both human and universal. We are here to learn how to reunite with love's healing energy.

It is crucial for each human being to know love. This is what we are doing here on earth: learning about love. William Blake said, "And we are put on earth a little space/ To learn to bear the beams of Love."

Through human love, you learn about attachment, and this is where the pain comes in. But bonds of attachment come as teachers, as gifts in disguise, to help you to grow and learn more about yourself.

You are also learning about self-acceptance, self-love. You could love yourself infinitely if you remembered that at your core is this loving energy. As a creature of the universe, you're here as a part of nature, a part of the infinite energy. Even if you've made mistakes in your life, you still deserve the greatest love and self-acceptance. The same molecules of life energy that vibrate within you are vibrating within everyone and everything else as well, and so you're an important part of the ever-vibrating energy of the entire universe. This is why it is so important to honor and respect yourself. You have a purpose in this universe, and you have your own beauty, your own dignity, your own greatness. You are here for some reason—and, even though you may have flaws and imperfections, it is still important to honor and to love yourself.

Healing is about remembering these truths. When you are out of harmony with them, then illness and pain can set in. Then you are at odds with your own being. Sometimes, illness or pain is an attempt to get this love for yourself. It is sometimes a deeply embedded wish for nurturing, parenting, affection, and approval. Sometimes it is about being out of the "vibration of love"—in which case the molecules of your body are vibrating in anger or in confusion or grief. Healing is about remembering who you really are.

Finding Your Essence

If you look beyond your personality, your everyday difficulties, your public faces, you will find your essence. It has qualities of love and strength and peace, although it is really none of these qualities, but an all-pervading energy. To truly know it, it is most often necessary to go within through meditation, hypnosis, contemplation, or prayer; but you can experience it at any moment as you go about the course of your life.

And no matter what you have been through in your lifetime—no matter how unworthy you feel, or how much guilt you may be dragging along, or how many times you feel you have failed—there is an inner core beyond all of this drama of life. Your personality is only one level of your identity. The essential level is your inner core, and it is who you are in the most fundamental way.

You get cut off from your natural self at an early age, and you forget what's there at your nucleus. You believe your own story. You think you're the one who has failed at relationships, the one who has made so many mistakes, the one who has been so badly abused or who abuses. This is your surface self, and it is important because it is your opportunity for learning. It is your vehicle for operating in the world. But you need to define yourself more broadly and to remember your love, power, energy, and creativity—and to extend these naturally healing elements to those parts of yourself that are in need of healing. It might help you to recall particular times you felt especially strong, creative, loving or peaceful, as these are reflections of essence.

"There is a reason for everything, a perfection to everything, a beauty of form for everything. Your life isn't just random. There's a great plan and a plan for your personal evolution. In difficult times, the perfection may be hard to see, but there will come a day when the meaning will open up before you and show you the necessity of your suffering."

SamuEl

The
Healing
Attitudes

Sometimes healing means an actual change in a condition. It may be a change in a physical condition, like tumors or back pains or blood pressure. Or it may mean that you've been able to overcome a habit, such as overeating or biting your nails or ingesting harmful substances. Sometimes it means a shift in an emotional condition—coming to terms with early abuse, stabilizing yourself after a loss in relationship, handling the fear of closeness with another.

Healing also means that you've made a significant shift in perception, in creating a new perspective. Hypnotherapy helps first of all by bringing you, through the trance state, to another level of your being so that you can view things differently. The process then works step by step to help you shift the way you've been looking at your early life, your present reality, and your future possibilities. Healing means that you change your attitudes.

What are the Healing Attitudes?

• LIFE IS LEARNING.

It is true—we have come here to this earth to have experiences of learning. Some of us are learning about physical illness; others about what it is like to live in poverty or riches; still others have come to learn about being victims or victimizers. We can make decisions about how we react to these experiences, whether we use them for growth or oppression.

Wounds have value. You don't have to rush in and heal them, but savor the lessons and discover the purpose of the wound—and then look toward healing.

• WE ARE EVOLVING.

Through lesson after lesson, we are becoming, individually and collectively, more enlightened.

Understanding this helps you to see how, in relationships, for example, you may be dealing with parents or siblings or children who are at different stages from you. This is not a value judgment, but an opportunity to accept others at whatever stage they may be working in at a given moment in time. It's also an opportunity to accept and respect your own self at whatever stage you are in now, knowing that it is inevitable that you will grow.

• ROOTS OF CHILDHOOD WOUNDS IN PRESENT PROBLEMS CAN BE HEALED.

It is only human to re-create past hurts in current relationships. You can come to terms with this by first experiencing these problems and unfulfillments, then seeing how they are reappearing in your present situation, and then allowing your essence to heal them.

• IT IS POSSIBLE TO SHIFT YOUR REALITY.

It is possible, for example, to see the advantage in everything, to see how the fall you took on the stairs gave you the time you needed to rest or to go within. Or to see how the loss of your relationship gave you the chance to grow and expand. Or how the abuse you received gave you compassion for others who also have difficulties.

It is possible to alter the way you perceive your childhood, your relationships, your work. As you read on, you'll find stories about these internal shifts.

• IT IS POSSIBLE TO SHIFT YOUR CONSCIOUSNESS LEVEL.

We are all electromagnetic, and we vibrate at various frequencies. Vibrating at higher rates will make you like a tuning fork, attuned to more rarified levels, levels in which you become more in touch with essence. When you do shift your rate of vibration and your consciousness, you are able to experience old negativities in different ways, not identifying so much with them, but being able to see and then transform them.

• YOU DESERVE TO BE LOVED AND HEALED.

When you're not used to being loved well, you think you might have done something to create that situation, and so maybe you don't merit happiness or a good life. Sometimes you beat up on yourself for this reason; that's also what you're used to, and, for some strange reason, that's your comfort zone. If you were good and worthy, you think you'd have had two great loving parents, enough of everything, smooth sailing all through your life. But the truth is that your life experiences are your teachings, and their difficulty does not reflect your own merit. You have true worth; you are essence, and you are connected with every living thing in the universe. You deserve healing and love and all good. And even if the light may seem frightening at times, it is still your birthright to be able to live in it.

• YOU CAN MAKE A DECISION TO HEAL YOURSELF.

This "healing decision" is crucial in any attempt to shift your conditions. It comes from deep within, when you've "had it" with some situation, "had it" to the point that you're unwilling to let it go unhealed any longer. This may come as some internal "click" inside of you, the "I'm ready!" state that everyone who is ready to stop drinking or smoking or participating in abusive relationships knows so well.

It is difficult to heal without getting to this state. Up to that point, there is usually denial that the problem even exists. But the time comes when it seems as if the tree in the forest is ready to fall on you, and that's the time you know you've got to move.

• THERE IS A PLACE OF LOVE AND UNDERSTANDING WITHIN YOU.

This, again, is essence. It is the deep strength and wisdom of your soul, the experience of "I am", and getting back there is what healing is all about. You can hold your issues of personality in the light and transform them with wisdom, shed the light of awareness on the dark places within you. You go directly to this place of love and awareness and heal all other parts of your being.

"Allow your love to stream forth.
Find the deeply recessed place in yourself that is so
magnanimous and embracing that it even embraces
all your difficulties. In that openness of your heart,
you can melt away the dark feelings
you have held so dear."

SamuEl

Healing with
Essence Hypnotherapy:
How It's
Done

If you're not a hypnotherapist, I don't expect that after reading this section, you're going to sit down and use all of these techniques—although you might. My purpose here is to show you just how this work is done. A great deal of it can be adapted for work on yourself. Sometimes just reading about the techniques will bring healing experiences for you. These are thumbnail sketches of much more complex processes that can be used in hypnotherapy or in self-hypnosis, and reading it will give you information that will help you understand more clearly the healing stories that follow.

Discovering the Problem

Just what is it that you want to heal? Sometimes it's very clear; you want to heal a fear of earthquakes, a lack of finances, a relationship rut, a pain in the lower back, an addiction to candy bars. Sometimes you just feel a sense of malaise, and you know that life can be better. It is important to get very clear about what you would like to do, and then you can begin. If you're not certain what the main issue is, then you can either find someone who can help you clarify it, or you can get a paper and pencil, and write on it: "I would like to heal...", and then you write whatever comes into your mind. Be as specific as you can, describing the problem and how it affects your life.

Trance

When you are ready, a hypnotherapist will induce a trance, or you can do self-hypnosis. Trance is a state of altered consciousness, a state of deep relaxation, and going into trance is one way of reaching your essence. There are thousands of ways to induce it. You may have seen hypnotists inducing trance with pendulums or spiraling discs, but many hypnotherapists simply use their voices in soft and relaxing ways. Here are a few commonly used trance induction methods; remember that the possibilities are endless:

> Breathe deeply and pay attention to your
> breathing....
> Count down from 30 to 1 (or more or less,
> depending on how long you need)....
> Imagine a beautiful place, and relax there....
> Imagine a hammock, and swing on it....
> Relax the various parts of your body, beginning
> with your feet....
> Say, "Relax now. Go deeper and deeper now."....
> Imagine walking downstairs and going more
> deeply as you walk....
> Imagine floating in the sky or on the water....
> Use a natural scenario that relaxes you deeply.

If you are doing this on your own, it may help to use a cassette tape. You can make one for yourself or use one that has already been made for this purpose. You'll find a full trance induction in the last part of this book, and you can feel free to use it to make a tape for yourself.

Trance is a very natural state that is comfortable and pleasant. You have experienced it many times when you've focused your mind. You have felt it in those moments before falling asleep, when part of you is almost awake and another part of you is floating off into dreamland. You've experienced trance while watching a movie or TV when you're focused on what you're watching and become completely absorbed in it, almost forgetting that there is another reality. Trance is a perfect way to experience your essence; your everyday mind is quiet, and your deepest being can shine through when you fully and totally relax.

Healing Yourself as a Child

This is a rich and fertile ground for healing. Reading the examples of inner child healing elsewhere in this book can show you how this can be an extraordinary healing vehicle. In trance, you go back to a picture of yourself as a child—at any age that your consciousness would like to show you. When you see the child, there are many things you can then do. You can observe the child for as long as you need and want to. You can bring yourself in as an adult to hold and stroke the child and give her love. You can play with her—whatever she likes to do—or you can walk together in favorite places. You can imagine the healing light or healing water helping the child. You can give the child a new set of parents. And you can rescue the child from her circumstances and take her into a new environment—even home with you!

Here's what an inner child session with a hypnotherapist might be like:

"Just go back now and see yourself as a child, at any age that your subconscious mind would like to show you. Do you see her?"

"Yes, she's sitting on a big chair with her dolls."

"How old is she?"

"She's six."

"What does she look like?"

"She's has dark curls, and she's not very big. She looks sad."

"What's she sad about?"

"No one is around, and she wonders where everyone is."

"Where is everyone?"

"Her mother is working, and her father isn't there, and maybe her grandmother is there, but she's very busy."

"How does the little girl feel?"

"She wants to cry." She begins crying now.

"Do you know that there is someone who would love to be with her and to give her love ? Why don't you bring yourself in as an adult and hold her?"

"She's glad I'm here now. She doesn't want to cry now."

"Maybe you can tell her that you'll be there for her when she needs you."

"Yes, I will. She's very happy that she's with me."

"That's right; she's made a special connection with you, and you're someone who can really understand her. It changes her life to know that you're around."

Sometimes you can become the child and experience her feelings. Because the child is so close to essence, meeting her will help you to unite with this tender and wonderful part of your own being.

Subpersonalities

These are different parts of your being that appear in your life as characteristic behaviors. Some common ones are The Critic or The Judge, The Perfectionist, The Angry One, The Sad One, and, of course, The Inner Child in all of its varieties. In hypnosis you can find your own indiosyncratic parts. If you assume that these subpersonalities exist, you can work beautifully with them in trance. These are not separate personalities, as in multiple personalities, but parts of yourself that get triggered by various life situations. You also assume that there is a loving, centered part of your being that supercedes all the subpersonalities and can heal them and make them whole. You assume that this exists in everyone and that it is easily experienced in the trance state.

Subpersonalities are usually trying to do something that they consider positive for you—although it more often than not turns out to be quite the opposite. For example, The Hungry One may be eating and eating in a way that it thinks is protecting and comforting you—but, in actuality, it may be harming you even more. In hypnosis, you can find out what the subpersonality is doing, and you can give it something else to do—something more useful and beneficial and in harmony with your real needs. You can also exaggerate this subpersonality, almost to the point of caricature—and you can see some of your behaviors with greater clarity. This may even make you laugh when you see it behaving in exaggerated form. There are many more ways you can deal with subpersonalities—and there are many wonderful books you can read on the subject. Essence Hypnotherapy emphasizes that the healthy loving aspects of the being can heal the other less functional ones.

Here's what a subpersonality might look like in hypnotherapy:

"Just go inside now and find the part of yourself that likes to overeat bread."

"It's a blob. It's name is 'the Blob'. I want to cry now, but I can't."

"Why not?"

"The Blob is in the car with my mother, and my mother is yelling at it, but she won't let it cry."

"How does that Blob feel?"

"It feels shame, humiliation. It feels like it wants to cry but can't. It feels like it needs someone to give it love. Now it's eating bread. That makes it feel more comfortable."

"Would you like that Blob to be able to feel more love and eat less bread?"

"Yes!"

At this point, you bring in love from your strong and integrated self, from a special loving figure, or from essence, itself. You can suggest that when this desire to eat all the bread in the world comes up that now you can be more conscious of what is going on, and you can do something else that is truly nurturing, something far more nurturing than eating bread.

The important point here is that there is that part of you that is already healed, your essence, that can bring healing to all other parts of your being.

Seeing Parents as Children

If you are ready for this (that is, if you've done some preliminary healing work on your own self), you can go back to a time when your parents were children and see what forces created them to be the kind of people that they are now. You can get in tune with your intuition if you have no idea about your parents' childhood, and you can see pictures of what your father's or your mother's childhood was like. This helps you to understand the human weaknesses of your parents; it also helps to give you some feeling for their motivations for being the way they are.

You can also stand back and envision your parents as separate human beings, coming to this earth to work out whatever they came to work out; they are toiling and suffering like everyone else—some of them stuck in ignorance, some in anger, some in servitude— whatever they may be working out. Understanding this may help you to make a separation from them in your consciousness. You are not just their "child". You are fellow beings who've come to this earth together to learn. Seeing your parents this way is liberating.

It's actually comforting to know that you really aren't their "child" anymore; nor are you their "victim".

You happened to come to this earth together to work things out, and now that you see them more clearly, you can take responsibility for your own healing, and get on with it. You also realize that you don't have to take responsibility for healing them, only if it is requested and you're willing.

This doesn't mean that you have to condone all of your parents' behavior. This doesn't mean that you have to accept abuse or mistreatment if you have experienced it in your life. What this does mean is that you are able to stand back and see your parents from another perspective. Something changes inside of you when you see your parents as separate beings who are struggling to comprehend what life is about. When you get the message about this, some of the resentment can drop away, especially when you see how your early life was a true learning experience.

One woman had a mother who was unaffectionate and rigid. Once when she was a girl of five, she was in the hospital with a broken leg. In hypnosis she remembered that her mother had paid her little attention; she had been unfeeling and remote. I asked her to imagine what her mother had been like at age five. She saw that her mother had been the youngest child in an unhappy family, brutalized by her father and siblings. As an adult, she had gone dry, and she had no love to give. Seeing this helped the daughter to realize that she was really worthy of love, but her mother just hadn't been able to give it. Now she was able to stop wishing to get "blood out of the turnip" that her mother had become, and she realized that the source of love was really deep within herself.

Asking Guidance for Answers

If you are concerned about a current decision—(perhaps you are at a crossroad or in some type of quandary)—or you simply would like to get in touch with your Higher Guidance, trance is an excellent vehicle. In a state of deep relaxation or self-hypnosis, you open yourself for guidance to come from deeply within. You may pose a question. It may be, "What is my next step?" And you wait to receive a picture or phrase that gives you a hint about what your next step may be. You can write down or tape your answers. (See "Hypnotic Writing" for pointers on how to do this.) You might ask for guidance about a current relationship, a career decision, a financial problem. The more you do this, the more adept you become. You learn to trust your guidance, and you also see how much it is supporting you.

In a session, the hypnotherapist might say, "You can open yourself now to bring forth inner guidance that will help you understand your situation more fully." Sometimes your answers will be short and general, such as, "You are going in the right direction. You will find what you are looking for. Be strong, have patience and fortitude, and the seeds you have planted will flower." Some answers are more detailed, telling you in great detail what is happening in your relationships, your checkbook, your work life, and then telling you what you need to do to improve them.

So often we are inclined to seek outside of ourselves for answers to our problems. You will be amazed to see how these answers can come from your own wisdom. You'll find more on this in the chapter called "What You Can Do On Your Own".

Paying Attention to Body

As you work in trance, you will have various bodily reactions. You may feel a tightness in the chest or a pain in the abdomen when you experience some of the discomforts that are within. It is advisable to explore these experiences rather than to ignore them, for they are often rich in metaphor, and as you explore them, they change of their own accord. So when you take a look at the discomfort in your solar plexus, for example, you may find that there's something for you that is hard to stomach. What is this sensation telling you? You can watch it transform as you work with it. It is important to remember that not all bodily reactions are metaphoric. Some are strictly physiological. A stomach talking in trance, though it may mean that you are releasing and letting go, may also mean that you are hungry!

One woman felt that she had been rejected by her old boyfriend, and in trance, her stomach began to hurt. She said it felt like a knife was in there. I asked her to go in there and see what was there. It was a dark, murky, wet, stone dungeon. I asked her what was in there. She saw children in the schoolyard rejecting her because she was different. We plucked out that memory as if we were doing "psychic surgery". I asked her what else was there. She saw her old boyfriend rejecting her. We plucked this out also; we took these incidents out one by one and looked at them differently.

"You are not unworthy," I said. "People may not understand you, but you are not unworthy."

By going into that pain in her stomach, she had confronted the darkness until it became lighter and lighter, and then she was able to come out on the other side of it. As we pulled out past events and re-understood them, she was able to see her current experience more clearly. And the pain in her stomach had gone.

Paying Attention to Feelings

As you work with deep issues, you notice that emotions come forth quite easily. Often people cry in trance—even if there is no overt sadness. Trance is so relaxing, that it invites discharge of all kinds—including tears and deep-seated emotions. If you allow them in an atmosphere of tenderness, these too will change. You need to keep a lot of tissues on hand and let the feelings flow. Allowing and embracing their release will pave the way for their eventual transformation.

Communications You Need to Make

When you're in trance, you often find that you want to say something to someone who has been important to you in your life. This person may have treated you with love or with cruelty. He or she may or may not still be alive. This may be a family member or a teacher or a lover. In trance, you can make these communications safely. They may lead to actual communication—or the trance experience may be enough. You may want to say things to them out loud, or you may want to experience the communication silently. Or you can write these communications in hypnotic writing. Whatever may be the mode you choose, you will find it a relief to communicate whatever you have been keeping inside for so long.

One man, after working in trance on the violence that his father had perpetrated on the family, began to speak to his father. He began to speak to him completely in Spanish, for that was all that his father could understand. Later he translated it, "Dad, your anger has hurt me and mother and the other children also. It has hurt us, but we are all healing ourselves now." He felt very powerful after he expressed this in trance. Later he said this was the most fluent Spanish he had ever spoken.

Pulling Out Cords

If you have been tied to someone psychically or psychologically for a long time, you may be feeling restrictions from this relationship. You can imagine a cord that is attaching you to this person, and you can rip it out, just the way a switchboard operator used to pull the plugs. Or you may choose to cut the cords with scissors instead. The cords can be attached in various places—usually corresponding to the chakras or energy centers (see Ball of Light process). The most usual places in which cords are attached are the heart center and the solar plexus.

If you feel that someone is trying to control you or to take over your energy, you can also protect yourself in other ways in trance. You can imagine a shield of golden drops of light or of golden mesh net all around yourself, and you can declare yourself inviolable.

Outgrowing It

After you have done work with the child you once were or with some of the subpersonalities, the hypnotherapist can say to the adult, "You are not that child (or that personality) anymore. You're grown now, and you don't need to carry that burden with you any longer. You are free now." This statement, communicated to the subconscious, has a powerful effect of sealing the transformational work you are doing.

Healing with Touch

In hypnosis, as in everyday consciousness, it is often beneficial to be touched—usually on the forehead, the shoulders, the hands and arms, the heart center, and the solar plexus. It is good to be touched lovingly, from the heart—not clinically. Touch helps especially when you are working with the inner child. It is nurturing and healing and serves to help you to feel a sense of comfort and caring.

It is also worthwhile to be "touched without touching". This means that your energy field is "touched" by hands stroking the air above your body, in slow stroking motions or in slow circular movements. This has a very healing effect, and it helps you to get into trance more deeply as well as to feel a sense of wholeness.

Healing with Light

This is a technique that can integrate you after you have been in pain or after you have gone through a healing process. Healing with Light is actually more than a technique. It is a way of directly experiencing the Healing Presence or Higher Power or essence. You can imagine that a beam of light is coming to you from a place in the universe or from another being— or that this beam of light is coming from within as a radiance emanating from yourself, illuminating you from the inside out. If it is a beam of light coming from a source other than from inside of you, you can imagine that it is a spotlight or a sunbeam. You can imagine that it is beaming on you directly, healing every cell of your body and every bit of your mind. You can also imagine it emanating from another person or being—a healer or a special being—or from someone you know and love. And, of course, it can come from inside yourself because you have this healing essence within you.

Healing with Water

Water is a basic element of your being. It composes a major percentage of your chemical makeup. It was your early fetal environment; it grows life and it also destroys life. It has great healing and transformative powers, on both physical and inner levels. Water visualizations can wash clean old emotions, and can regenerate bodies and spirits as well. You can imagine that you are in a pool of water, a waterfall, a pond—or even the ocean, and you are washing away negativity, illness and pain. If you have a fear of water, you need only wade in or splash the water on yourself. If you are an enthusiast, you can dive in and explore the depths of the ocean, glide past the undersea ocean life, and clear away your difficulties. You can clean the dirt of childhood abuse or the pain of anger, fear, guilt, and grief.

Regression

There are many ways of experiencing regression in trance. One is to simply go back and re-experience an event from the past. This may be useful to you if you would like to get some information. You may want to visit your inner child this way or to re-live something that took place in the life of a family member.

If you have a pain, you may want to go back to earlier and earlier experiences of this pain, and you may reach the point of origin. This can be helpful if you are looking for the moment when a particular condition or event or feeling originally occurred.

You may also want to "re-paint your past". This means that you can alter the details of an experience so that you can heal. This doesn't mean that you're whitewashing over the truth. This may mean that you are bringing healing, caring, and love into the past, so that the present can be experienced with more love as well. You may also want to rescue someone (maybe even yourself) from some distress of the past. You can even administer trauma care.

"Past Life Regression" is another possibility in trance. Some people take this quite literally, and others experience it as a metaphor. For example, if in trance you go to an event that is not from your current frame of reference, you may experience it as another lifetime—or you may experience it as an important healing metaphor for you, and you can find healing in it. For example, if you are wondering why your throat hurts so often now, you may go to another country and another time where your throat was hurt. This may be an opportunity for you to heal the pain. You can take this experience metaphorically if you like—or you can take it at face value.

One man had a difficult relationship with his grandmother. He remembered a time when he was little that he and his twin brother were crying, and his grandmother only picked up his brother. She had told him, a little boy of three, that he was "faking it", and he wasn't going to get picked up. He felt hurt and angry, and he decided he wanted to do some past life regression to find out more about his relationship with his grandmother. He decided on some mode of transportation to take him back there. He chose a ship, and as I counted from ten to one, he sailed in his ship across the waters to another land. At the count of one, he landed, and got off the ship.

"Where are you now?" I asked him.

"I'm standing on some barren soil. There are dead

leaves on the ground, and I feel disappointed and dejected."

"What do your shoes look like?" I asked.

"They're raggedy and old," he answered.

I asked him what had happened.

"I owe money. I'm a debtor, and I can't pay, so I gave them my son," he answered tearfully.

"So how does your grandmother fit in here?" I asked.

"She was my son!" was his answer. He felt it in his body as an intense pressure.

So this was his grandmother's way of paying him back in another lifetime. She had been the son he had given away to pay back a debt. Now whether this was metaphorical or actual, it helped him to let go of his anger at this grandmother for her very conditional love.

Witness Consciousness

Much of the time, most people are so deeply embroiled in their life situations that they become victims of these situations, on a wheel of life that is going round and round, locked in the cogs of the wheel, spinning endlessly through patterns, beliefs, old behaviors. When you are in witness consciousness, you are able to step off the wheel for that moment and see yourself as you really are. You are an objective observer. It is often easier in trance to watch yourself with objective awareness than it is in your everyday state. In trance you can see yourself with more clarity and with a less subjective point of view. You may be able to watch your own situation as you would watch a drama on stage. With this panoramic perspective, you may feel as if you have a lighter load to carry. Using your natural ability, you stand back and observe.

So you may be crying, for example, and you might be watching yourself cry at the same time. While you're expressing yourself, you're also able to observe more objectively what is making you cry, how it feels for you to do it, what it means to you. The advantage of this is that you don't become so embroiled in your own processes. You are in your emotions, but you are not controlled by them. In the same way, you can be a part of your life's dramas, but you are not a victim of them.

Mind-Body Healing

Body and mind are intricately connected, and it is often fascinating in trance to see just how these connections are made. Someone may, for example, see that a rash on her skin is connected to emotions that may be "breaking out" from the inside. Trance can help you to see these connections more easily. Again, not every physical symptom can be understood this way, however. Some rashes, for example, are caused by environmental chemicals, not inner conflicts. So it's important to be wise about how far you go with this way of thinking.

Golden Ball of Light

This is another way to clear and cleanse and purify yourself. You imagine a radiant, scintillating ball of light vibrating and turning just above your head in your seventh chakra, or energy center. The ball now descends into your forehead (your sixth chakra) where it vibrates and enhances your ability to experience your own wisdom. It descends some more now, down into your fifth chakra, your throat, where it cleanses and purifies your ability to communicate. It then goes into your heart center, your fourth chakra, vibrating and spinning and cleansing your ability to experience love and compassion. Now it moves into your solar plexus or third chakra, where it enhances your ability to experience your own personal power and feelings. And then the second chakra, the genital area, where it cleanses and heals your sexuality, and down to your first chakra at the base of the spine, where it strengthens and heals your ability to survive with ease. Next it moves down your legs and out your feet like a fountain of light. As it moves out of your feet, it begins to travel upward again, up the sides of your body and back into the top of your head, over and over, cleansing and clearing you.

Visualizations like these, done in trance states. help to activate your natural inner healing powers.

Trance Rehearsal

This is also called "future pacing"—and it is often valuable for rehearsing a behavior or an activity before it is actually played out in life. You may want to practice being a non-smoker, speaking with ease in front of an audience, telling a parent that you are gay, or healing a serious illness. You use this technique quite naturally all the time—but in trance it is even more powerful because you are so relaxed and receptive.

This is an ideal way to help you overcome fear—to go driving before you actually have to get on the freeway if you are afraid or to go up the elevator of the tall building that scares you. It is also one good way to break a habit, seeing yourself, for example, free of biting your nails in every possible old nail-biting situation.

If this sounds to you like creative visualization—it is. Doing visualization while deeply in trance can be very powerful.

Posthypnotic Suggestions

We all know what these are—and for good reason. They are potent. Since children are naturally in trance so much of the time, the remarks you make to them often become posthypnotic suggestions. If you say to a child, "You'll never amount to anything." —or "You are so creative."—these comments will become embedded in the subconscious, and they will be posthypnotic suggestions that they will carry with them into adulthood.

In trance, you are naturally suggestible; you can make and receive suggestions easily. Some people are afraid to use these for fear of being too authoritarian or directive. On the contrary, if the chosen suggestions are in harmony with an individual's needs, trance may be a perfect opportunity for suggestion-making. "You are healing rapidly now, and you are finding no traces of your cancer." or "You are finding that your job interview is relaxed and easy." or "You are now a non-smoker, and you never want or need to smoke again." are examples of appropriate posthypnotic suggestions. Suggestions given with intention can work beautifully to bring forth the experience of healing.

Techniques for Pain

There are many techniques for dealing with pain. One method of alleviating physical pain is to observe it and experience it as an object. You take note of its color, its size, its shape, its weight, its location. You may even want to imagine the pain decreasing by ascribing a color to it (or a shape) and by imagining that it is growing lighter in color and smaller in size. Perhaps it is a giant throbbing orange ball at first; then it grows smaller and peach-colored. Then it is pink and very small, and then it becomes a tiny blue dot and disappears through one of the passageways of the body. It can float out your ears, your fingertips, or it can fall like rain out of the bottoms of your feet.

Another way to handle your pain once you have experienced it as fully as you believe to be possible, is to anesthetize it through the power of your mind. Put your hand on it, and imagine that you are applying an anesthetic—or just do so with your mind. Or tell another, "I am applying a topical anesthetic to your discomfort, and now I am injecting the anesthetic inside." Or you can put your hand on the pain and say, "My hand is a magnet, and your discomfort is being magnetized to it just as if it were made of iron filings." or "My hand is a sponge, and it is absorbing your discomfort, just as a paper towel absorbs ink."

You may not want to make your pain disappear at all; it may be instructive for you if you allow yourself to become as fully aware of it as you can.

Experiencing Essence

When you go inside to the deepest places within, you experience essence as the underlying core of your being. Sometimes you have to peel away obstructions to its experience, but you will find it. It is your birthright to know your essence, and it is the ultimate experience of healing.

"It is your birthright to know the infinite love that is within you, and when you experience it, you can walk with love amidst the turmoil of the world."

SamuEl

Getting
Ready for
a Session

"I'm feeling really nervous," Joan admitted as she sat down across from me.

"This will be the most relaxed you've ever been, "I reassured her.

She had never been hypnotized before, and she had visions of Svengali with his pendulum and his riveting gaze.

I sat across from her, and I talked with her about the lack of rain and the warmth of the day and whether or not she'd like some water or some tea. We were going to do some deep work together, and I wanted us to establish rapport. I talked with her about her family and her sprained ankle and then her reason for coming to see me. She had a problem with sweets; she couldn't stop eating them.

I asked her how long the problem had been going on.

"Three years," she answered. " Before that I never cared much for them."

"What happened three years ago?" I asked.

She pondered this question for a while, and I saw a flash of recognition come over her as she replied, "That's when my mother died, and that's when my marriage started to go downhill." As obvious as this may seem, it had not been quite so obvious to Joan who had never connected these incidents. Sometimes we miss what's happening up close.

She had had a deep connection with her mother, and the depression and grief she felt when her mother died changed her so drastically that she was a different woman to her husband. When their communication stopped, she began to eat every sweet thing in sight.

"Perhaps we can take a deeper look at this in hypnosis," I suggested. "And maybe we can do some healing."

She was beginning to relax. Her eyes brightened; her breathing was easier.

"What is the trance state that you told me I'd get into?" she asked.

"Trance is a state of altered consciousness," I told her. "It's similar to sleep—except that you're more aware. Your critical mind is quiet for a while, and you become more open to a profound kind of relaxation. You've experienced this before in one way or another—perhaps when you became so engrossed in a movie that you forgot everything around you or when you remembered your trip to the ocean in a daydream. If you've ever done meditation or visualization or relaxation, you have some experience of trance."

Her eyes were beginning to soften; her arms and legs were letting go of tension as we talked.

"When you relax this way or go into trance," I went on, "you can begin to heal yourself. You reach into a place that's already healed and full of love within yourself."

"Well—I don't know, " she was becoming skeptical again. "I don't know about that place you're talking about."

"Underneath your pain and grief and anger and fear there is love—and you can find it when you first experience your feelings and then penetrate even more deeply within where you can find the healing essence inside yourself."

She decided to suspend her disbelief, and she was ready now to go within. After we talked together for a while longer about her situation, we began her trance induction and her healing experience.

On the pages that follow, you'll be able to read what we actually did in sessions like Joan's, and you'll find issues that most of us are grappling with—such as

love and childhood and habits and pains and fears—
and how some people have learned to heal them.

So—just let yourself relax and take a deep breath
in, and enjoy the experiences of healing by
remembering who you are.

"No matter what you have been told or what you think of yourself, you are worthy of the greatest love. Within you is divinity and true inner worth."

SamuEl

Some Healing Stories

How Hypnotherapy Can Be Used in Specific Situations

Healing Food and Eating Problems

Meredith regularly ate junk-food—cookies, cakes, caffeine, sodas—and at times she stuffed herself beyond the point of no return. She knew that she was destroying her health, and she desperately wanted to change these habits. But it had always been a great struggle; she was hooked.

She came to hypnotherapy after she had tried just about everything else. We sat and talked for a while, and when she was ready we did a trance induction. I asked her to go back to a time, anytime, that had made an impact on her eating habits. I told her that her subconscious mind would know just which one would be important.

Her mind took her to a time when she was a little girl of four years old, and her parents were hugging her, but she didn't feel any love from their hearts. Her father and brother teased and humiliated her. She felt empty and unloved. Seeing this picture helped her to remember, but there was another part of her that was watching the scene. With her mature mind, she now understood that her mother and father felt "empty" to her, not because she didn't deserve love, but because they were missing love in their own lives, and they simply didn't have enough to give. She had always thought that she'd done something wrong, that she didn't deserve to be loved, but now she knew the real reason.

I asked her to find another picture. She went to a time when she was ten, and she was sitting at the table eating chocolate cake. Her mother had always given her this when she was good (or when she hadn't been bad). The cake tasted so great! Her mother made it, and the sugar was love from Mom. It felt good; you knew she liked you if you could have dessert or treats. She desperately wanted to please her Mom, and eating her cake pleased her. She was happy eating that cake, and life was okay. She now saw how much the sugar was related to mother-love.

In another session, she went forward many years, and she saw a picture of her boyfriend leaving her for another woman, and now she realized that she had been "eating herself up" about this for years in order to fill the gaping holes. She was having many revelations, wisdom fom her essence that was helping to heal her.

I asked her to find parts of herself that were related to old habits she wanted to change. Inside she found an Old Man who had had one disappointment after another and who saw only the bleakness of life. Her throat was tight, and she could barely speak. Worries were in there, and she began to take them out one by one and put them in her cupped hand. "Here's the first one,"she said, "'Nothing is all right.' And the next: 'Life is not fair and no good.' And, 'What's the use?'" These were words that Meredith often heard from her father and also part of her own mind that she tried to stuff down with food.

I asked her if there were any other parts inside. She found a girl with a pink dress and long hair like Alice in Wonderland who liked to laugh and play. She flitted around like a flighty ballerina, giggling and dancing. This part of her was as strong as the Old Man, but it wasn't involved in self-destructive behavior at all; it was light and gentle and happy. Now she realized she could balance these parts more skillfully within herself.

Her essence could watch all the parts with objectivity—watch when the Old Man bemoaned the world, watch when the Laughing One felt light and free. She could see more clearly and not have to push any of them down with food. The witness consciousness of essence helped her to feel compassion and love for the cast of characters within herself.

In another session, we went back again to look at Meredith's early life. She was seven, and her baby brother was born. She felt so angry because her mother didn't give her enough love, and now that her brother was here Meredith had even less. No one paid attention to her anymore. She hated the new baby and felt guilty to have such terrible thoughts. She knew now that one of the reasons she ate junk was because she was angry at herself. I asked her if she'd like to help that little girl. She went to the seven year old, put her on her lap, and told her, "It's normal to feel the way you feel. It's okay to be angry. I love you." The two went out into the woods together to a special brook that she had loved as a child. They played with rocks and stones and looked at flowers, and the little one showed Meredith her favorite toys.

I asked her if there were any other pictures there in her mind. She found herself in the Garden of Eden walking along a path. It was warm, and there was a lot of fruit on the bushes and trees. There were the smells of ripe melon and pineapple. As she walked along the path there, she felt the sense of being unwanted, unloved, not good enough. She thought she didn't belong there, and she shouldn't eat those good fruits. She was ashamed of herself; she felt that if everyone knew what an unworthy person she really was, no one would like her anymore. As she saw this, the figure walking down the path changed. She became radiant and healthy, beautiful, sensitive, and loving, and she saw her innate worth.

I asked her if there were any voice that told her to

eat all the cookies she ate. She listened and heard it tell her, as it always did, "It won't matter if you eat these cookies. You're so bored, and so what if you eat these? They taste so good—and you need a reward, so go ahead." She said to the voice, "I'm not hungry." And the voice said, "Oh, that doesn't matter. Just go eat those cookies. It feels good."

I asked her to experience her strength now and to talk to that old compulsive voice. She told it, "I'm in charge now. There's no way you can get me to eat those cookies when I'm not hungry. *I* get to decide. I know you feel bored and empty and uncreative. I know you feel terrible about yourself. But you can be creative instead of destructive. You can find out what you want to create, and you can also begin to appreciate yourself. You can stop eating those cookies now."

In another session, I asked her to go to the place of guidance within herself to give herself some more understanding of her situation. Her essence spoke to her in the form of her inner wisdom, "You often eat when you are lonely. Your loneliness is a spur to help you grow. Blocking or numbing it with food only hinders you. Accept your loneliness, your boredom, your anger and your grief. Work with these feelings. Let yourself feel them, and then come back to the love."

I spoke to her deeper mind, and said, " You don't have to feed yourself junk anymore. When you were little, sugar was a reward. The people in your family showed their love through sweet food, but it's not a reward anymore. You can reward yourself in new ways now. You can give yourself love and nurturing. You can reward yourself by eating wholesome, healthy, delicious food in moderate amounts. You're not a little girl anymore, and the old ways are over. The rewards you get now are ten times greater. You deserve it, no matter how many things you did that weren't good. You deserve nurturing because you ARE, because your essence is goodness. When you trash your body, you're trashing a vehicle for essence to come into the world. You don't have a need anymore to trash your beautiful being."

She then got a spontaneous image of herself out on a cliff overlooking the ocean. She watched the waves roll onto the beach and out again. The clouds were floating peacefully above her. She felt a peaceful presence that brought her back to herself once again.

Finding a Greater Comfort

Eating is not only a necessity; it's a "comfort habit", a habit that seems to make you feel at ease and secure. Other such habits that seem to create comfort are smoking, drug-taking, overeating, junk eating, biting nails, twirling hair, and drinking. These habits are attempts to alter consciousness, to experience essence—mostly ill-fated attempts because of their negative side effects. Many of these are oral habits in which you are trying to fill that primal need of the infant in the arms of its mother, warmly sucking on her breast as she loves you in a peaceful idyllic way. You long for this ultimate satisfaction, for comfort and security and love. You long to be the infant at peace, and you seek to create that state by putting something into your mouth, into your body, to quiet your tension-filled mind. It seems to work for a short while, but it has long term repercussions and many negative effects.

Meredith looked for love from her parents, but when they hugged her, there was an empty feeling, and so she ate to fill the empty hole, to feel the safety and love she didn't feel as a child. The adults in her life (and in most of our lives) had little experience of their own essence. They never forged their own connections with their own essence, and so their heart centers were not open. So Meredith tried to fill the gap there with an easy-to-find oral gratification—food. The feeling of emptiness is also the sense of being separate from spirit.

Sugar to Meredith was an attempt to get the feeling of mother-love (as well as essence-love) again and again. She tried to fill the deep chasm so the feelings of separation from her essential self would go away. But the anguish and insecurity would only go away for a time. Meredith realized she needed to find a way to deal with her real issues: how she could feel less afraid and alone and more loved in some genuine ways.

As she remembered this abandonment by her old boyfriend, she saw how accurate the food metaphors are: She'd been "eating herself up', trying desperately to fill the empty space.

In meeting some of her subpersonalities, Meredith found the cynical Old Man and realized that she had been attempting to push this voice down, to "stuff away" her thoughts with food. She realized that she'd been pushing down feelings of anger, depression, and lack of love, and her fears of not being taken care of well enough. She's tried to alter her consciousness through food, and though she's masked the problem for a while, it is still always there. The food hasn't cured it.

She found the Playful Girl and realized that she could have access to more parts of herself. She also has access to essence, and that not only gives her joy, but it also helps her to be more objective so she can see all these parts of herself. She doesn't have to suppress anything to escape into temporary oblivion with food.

When she saw how she felt about the birth of her baby brother, Meredith realized the part that self-hatred had played in her food problems. She was stuffing away uncomfortable thoughts, feeding herself foods that she knew weren't really nourishing her, but still trying to get love and affection. In meeting her inner child, she was able to be the adult provider of this satisfaction. She validated the child by telling her that her anger was understandable, and then she comforted the child by giving her love.

In the Garden of Eden, Meredith confronted her issues of self-esteem. Is she good enough to eat the beautiful food, or does she really only deserve junk? Her shame is an important element here. She feels unworthy; she's done some terrible things (or so she believed), and she doesn't know if she's worthy enough to eat good healthy food. She was becoming aware of the fact that she has been identifying with false personality. This recognition brought her into contact with her essence.

She had also made a connection with her internal dialog and her own guidance by going into the trance state. She learned that she could talk to the voice that was bent upon destroying her. She realized that in her was the strength to confront that voice and assert that *she* was now in charge. She was also able to bring forth wisdom from within herself that told her not to cut off her difficult feelings through food—but to experience them and then let them go.

On a cliff, overlooking the ocean, she symbolically experienced essence. Most of us have profound experiences in natural settings. They evoke the inner experiences and also serve as outer symbols of essence. These outer experiences mirror our inner universes and provide powerful vehicles for healing.

The Healing Principles

- **You can find out what needs your food cravings are satisfying, and you can find more effective ways to get the satisfaction you deserve.**

    The roots of most food problems stem from basic human issues of love and self-esteem. Food is used to fill emptiness and loneliness, to mask self-hatred and shame, to find comfort and pleasure, to tranquilize, to avoid facing the light of essence—so many reasons. When you know of other ways to get your needs met and your problems solved, food ceases to be the only alternative.

- **You can see how feelings of lack of early nurturing may have contributed to food problems, and you can bring in the love of the present.**

    Not everyone has the experience of lack of early nurturing. Some people have a simple physiological addiction to sweets or carbohydrates or fats. But for others, the addiction is compounded with the satisfaction of these deeper needs. The primary principle here is that you have the capacity in adult years to bring to yourself what may have been missing earlier in your life.

- **You can experience how your subpersonalities are controlling your behaviors, and you can have more choice in your responses.**

    When you know it may be some "gremlin" or some lonely little kid that, as a part of you, is eating all those cookies, you get to make the decision about how you handle the matter. You can give the "gremlin" or the child some other way to play or get nurtured—and you can eat to satisfy a more evolved part of yourself. You can talk to these parts to remind them that they do not have the ultimate power over you.

- **You can center yourself in your essence and then eat with greater awareness of who you are really nourishing.**

"Part of our necessary development as human beings
is not only to have a great, loving, blissful heart; but also
to know it, to be aware of it, to recognize it fully....
Our full assignment in life, as human beings is, through
the suffering of separation, through the yearning for union,
to find it again...Through illuminating the situation
of this pain, this frustration this loss, this broken heart
from which everything begins—
we can become free."

Abbot Tenshin Reb Anderson

Healing Abandonment

Laura always felt that she had been abandoned—even though, for all practical purposes, her family was "intact". But she carried within her—actually in the pit of her stomach—a feeling of being left all alone. There were times when she cried on the slightest provocation, as if she were an infant.

In trance, we looked at some of the pictures about abandonment that she was carrying inside. She saw herself as an infant crying all night in her bed. Would no one pick her up? Where were they? Had they stayed asleep all night this time and left her all alone?

Next, she saw herself as a two year old in her playpen. Her mother was nowhere to be found—and no one came to get her. She was so terrified—not knowing if anyone would ever pick her up or take care of her again. She felt the full force of this terror. Then I asked her if she'd like to feel the love from the loving part of herself. She picked up the tiny infant from her crib and reminded her of this loving human mother-touch. She held the two year old and consoled her: "Your mother will be back soon. You don't have to worry. And I'm here now to keep you company, too."

Another time, she wanted to see if there were any past life connections to the abandonment feelings. In her mind she saw a peasant woman in a rural village. Her whole family had been killed, and she stood shocked and bereft, arms outstretched, face agonized, for now she was totally alone. She realized that she had been that woman, and she was now able to allow the healing power of her present strength to go to her and comfort her.

She wanted to go back even further. Now she found herself in a dungeon in Spain, and she was cold and hungry. She was gazing at the floor in a dazed stupor, wishing for some way out of this miserable hole. It was the time of the Spanish Inquisition, and she was to be put to death because of her unorthodox beliefs. I suggested that she find a place of courage within herself now and bring it to this woman, and now she was able to face her fate.

I asked her to recall other times she had felt this abandonment. She saw the first time she'd ever slept with a man—her first boyfriend—and a week went by before he called her. When he finally did, he told her, "I was afraid, so I left town for a while." And then she remembered her mother, lying on a bed depressed many times, telling her, "Go away. I don't want to be with you now." I then asked her to look at these incidents from a greater distance and with greater understanding. The first image she saw was of herself nursing herself as an infant at her own breast, and on her face was a knowing smile. She remembered that these old pictures of abandonment are images she had been carrying in her mind and that beyond them there is an experience of union. She remembered what a friend once told her: "I thank my mom and dad for never being there when I really needed them, because it eventually made me realize that what I really needed was myself." Laura feels her heart more opened by this healed state of love.

There is No Separation in Truth

Laura's family had felt "intact" to her on the surface—yet it suffered from numerous dysfunctions, not the least of which was the alcoholism of her father. Her mother, in fact, had had a breakdown, and this is why she was "away" when Laura was two. The neighbors had verified that when she was an infant she had cried all night long. Perhaps her parents had slept through it—but for her the reality was that no one had come and she had been left all alone.

Being able to go inside and bring love and comfort to these "abandoned" parts of her was the first step toward creating wholeness and reunification within herself. The next step was to experience herself as a strong being who had had experiences of abandonment—not an "abandoned person". This made all the difference as her self-concept began to change. And the step after this was to recognize that her essence is love and strength and that in remembering it, she could lift up all those lost parts of herself and give them the recognition of essence as well.

When Laura saw the peasant woman from a past life, it had a profound healing effect on her. Whether this was actually a past life or a metaphor of Laura's psyche was not important. She had been able to reach what seemed to be the roots of her affliction and to pull them up with the power of consolation and love.

She saw the prisoner, another past life metaphor, a symbol of her own constraint. She felt first-hand the freedom that came from within, no matter what the outer circumstance might be. She was also able to bring the experience of courage to a part of her psyche that was still there cowering in the corner of the dungeon. She had felt a tightness in her jaw and a gnawing in her belly; both of these subsided when she brought courage to a weaker part of herself.

Seeing the incidents of her boyfriend's and her mother's neglect gave her the opportunity to first of all remember the experiences, which is in itself liberating, and then reach beyond the experiences to an underlying truth that provided an opportunity for remembering her essence and the love that is there.

The Healing Principles

• *There is a well-developed part of you that can nurture the abandoned parts inside.*

> This part may be who you are now—a mature, loving individual who is able to give love to other parts of yourself. You may be more comfortable experiencing this nurturing from another, a loving person you know, a healer, a great being, or from a healing force in the universe. Whatever way you choose, the principle is clear: you have the capacity for bringing love into all parts of your being.

• *Past life experiences or personal metaphors can show you roots of problems.*

> Past-life healing experiences can be extraordinarily effective, whether or not you take them literally. One woman I worked with, for example, had a terrible pain in her throat. In a vision of a past life, she was being stabbed there by someone she presently knew. This vision completely eradicated the pain. It's like pulling weeds out of the ground by the roots.

• *The experiences of profound truth can help to heal the afflictions of a lifetime.*

> Most of the time, we don't see things as they really are. We live with veils covering our eyes. In special moments, the veils are lifted, and we see situations as we've never seen them before. This is always a great gift, always an act of healing.

"A sense of unworthiness does not make us unworthy.
It's been acquired over many lifetimes—if not
billions of mind-moments in this life—when we were told
or thought we were wrong or inadequate.
Everybody seems to have it to some degree....
We are worthy of letting go of our unworthiness....
Gently, with patience and a lot of love,
we acknowledge the being we really are."

Stephen Levine

Healing a Sense of Unworthiness

Paul got depressed a lot. He always had a big knot in his stomach, and he had an overriding feeling of not being at all worthwhile. His early life included some horrendous parental violence, and it left him a legacy of low self-worth.

We went into trance, and Paul went back directly to an old early picture. He saw himself as five years old. It was dinnertime, and his father was bashing him and the other kids, as he did almost every night. He and the other children were horrified by their father's anger. After Paul had experienced this as fully as he felt he needed to, I suggested that he bring in another influence. Now that he's grown and has the power of the present moment, he had the chance to escape from that family. He pictured himself as an adult rescuing the little boy who had decided to leave the family forever. In trance, he said to his father, "You never should have had children. You don't deserve them." Paul took the little boy over to his "junk drawer" to get some treasures to take away with him, and they went to a new home. Paul pulled out the sofabed for the boy and tucked him in for the night.

Paul saw another picture. It was Christmas eve, and Paul's father, in a blind rage, was killing the family cat. I suggested to Paul that he see his father as a little boy to see what he might have been like. Paul saw his father as a lonely, skinny, sickly little boy whose father had punished him unmercifully. Seeing his father's unhappiness gave Paul a chance to understand some of the roots of his father's behavior. I asked Paul if there were any places in his body where he felt particular connections with his father. He experienced some imaginary cords attaching the two of them at the forehead, the heart, and the solar plexus. Paul cut all the cords with the scissors of this mind, and the pain in his stomach subsided. He'd had this pain for a long time, and now it was gone.

Another time, I asked Paul to imagine what the part of himself that feels so unworthy might be like. He saw "Poor Paul", a part that was always feeling lousy about himself. Paul saw him larger than life. He had a hangdog expression, and he said, "I need to be taken care of. The world is too overwhelming. I think I'm going to go out and put a knife in my heart." The strong Paul, the part that was in touch with his essence, hugged him and protected him. I suggested that perhaps he'd like to feel the experience of healing light. He beamed the light on himself, feeling the warm beams bringing him in touch with the love and care of the universe.

I asked Paul to write about his feelings. He wrote: "Sometimes I get morose or depressed and think about killing myself, slashing myself up with a hunting knife or buying a gun to shoot myself. The fact is, I enjoy life too much to end it. There are so many incredible things to do and see in this world, and it may be kind of boring in the next one. There's travel and diving, and when I'm skiing down a mountain at top speed, I'm totally alive. There's gardening to do. And I want to see that new Woody Allen movie. Eventually I'll meet a woman who'll really love me, and I'll be really excited about her. Maybe I'm supposed to do some fantastic paintings or have a kid eventually who'll grow up to be a wonderful person. And what if I killed myself? I wouldn't want to lay that on the people in my life." Being in touch with warmth and with his true self was giving him a sense of the value of life.

In another session, I asked Paul to find within himself a powerful persona. He saw himself as a warrior-athlete playing soccer; that was him as his most vital self. He then imagined himself diving off a boat, pulling himself down on a piece of kelp, looking at sea snails, crabs, flounder—whole undersea communities of tiny animals and eco-systems. Diving helped him remember his power.

I asked him to look at the thoughts that were creating feelings of unworthiness in him : "She's not going to like me." or "I'm not going to be able to perform in bed." or "I can't get ahead financially." He saw origins in his being put in the "dumb row" at school, in his father's violence, in his brother's taunting him. He became the witness of his mind, and he saw the self-deprecation from a distance. Finally, he took responsibility for the thoughts and realized that they were his, and because he created them, he could also change them.

I also asked him if there were any way that his mind experienced the self-criticism most vividly. He imagined a "Committee" inside that was always criticizing him, telling him he's not attractive or smart. It was made up of all the teachers, parents, and relatives who, in Paul's eyes, had slighted or mistreated him. The committee read him "The Book of Rules", a book that had all the "do's and don'ts" of growing up and all the examples of how he never measured up, and with a fresh sense of being in control, he threw the book in the trash, and the committee became silent.

I asked him to see more images of his self-deprecation. He saw a long-haired chihuahua who wanted love and attention but got kicked away. His mature self saw that it's not because he's an unloveable dog—but it's that they weren't able to give him the love he needed. There are, however, sources that are more reliable; a new friend, a doberman, came to play, and he enjoyed its company.

He also saw himself as a turtle in the mud at the bottom of the water. He rose to the surface and sat on a rock in the light. Now another turtle came to sit beside him, and they basked together in the light.

He then found an image that to him mirrored his true self. He was sitting on a cliff overlooking the ocean. He felt complete here, as if some peaceful force, some presence had found its way to him and brought him back to himself.

Coming Out of the Mud

Paul has been constructing a whole new view of himself. His early experiences of violence and his self-effacing mind patterns have created feelings of unworthiness in him. Healing this is truly the work of a lifetime, and it can be done step by step, through validation, love, insight, and through connection with the true essential being.

Healing childhood traumas was a first step for Paul. It isn't always necessary to re-experience past events in order to heal; yet it is often transformative when you go back to these events with a healing attitude. In Paul's case, this meant, for example, that he could see his father's violence and know that he could now take the little boy out of that context. Paul returned to the childhood experience with an attitude of strength, with a part of himself that is already strong and intact that can heal the wounded parts.

When he severed the "cords" from himself to his father, Paul was obviously severing an "umbilical" connection. Severing the connection not only distanced him, but also released vital energy that had been blocked. Paul had been carrying the pain of his childhood as an actual physical pain in his body, which he was now able to release as he experienced the connection. When he saw his father as a "lonely, skinny, sickly little boy", Paul was again creating more distance, as well as more understanding. He was beginning to see the origins of his father's rage.

"Poor Paul" is a subpersonality that Paul had been dragging around inside of himself. Paul saw him as a caricature with sad eyes and a sense of being overwhelmed by everything. Seeing the caricature was a humorous experience for Paul, and it gave him the ability to laugh at this old stance of his. It is possible to heal a subpersonality by finding out what it has been needing (usually love or attention or validation)— and fulfilling those needs from your centered essence. There is always plenty of love there to give to disenfranchised parts of self.

As he became more centered in his essence, Paul was able to remember the value of his life and to make the decision to stay alive. By also experiencing the critical committee inside his mind, he was able to have greater objectivity and less identification with the committee's voices. Tossing away the "Book of Rules" was a conscious act of throwing off old, harmful systems of behavior.

As the chihuahua, he realized that he's loveable and that it's the problems of the other people in his life that have kept them from loving him. It's not because he's not worthy. This was a major realization for Paul. To add to this, he saw that all his life he had strived to please people, to be okay in their eyes, and now he realized that he already is worthy and loveable, and there was nothing that he needed to do or be to deserve love.

Seeing himself as the diver and feeling the power of that experience was very important. In hypnosis, another person experienced herself as she feels when she is doing martial arts; another as he is when performing on stage. These images of self are reflections of the connection with essence, and they can be helpful to trigger that remembrance.

When he experienced himself on the cliff overlooking the ocean, he felt a connection with his true self. He recognized this as the part of himself that is already healed and whole and perfect. From this vantage point, he realized that the whole issue of self-worth is an illusion, a long-lasting daydream. This deeper self is of the highest worth, always present, and the rest is a veil covering over the truth. Lifting the veil, then, is the work of a lifetime.

The Healing Principles

- **You can heal self-esteem issues by experiencing their origins in childhood patterns and in healing these roots.**

    There is always a healing element that you can bring to every event of your past. This element comes from within you, from the inner repository of your own essence.

- **You can "pull out cords" that connect you to the causes.**

    Often by detaching cords, you can de-emphasize unhealthy connections to others. It's like a telephone switchboard, with you the operator, inserting and pulling out connections wherever appropriate.

- **You can experience subpersonalities that often show up as humorous caricatures in order to help you become more objective about your situation.**

    When you blow up a subpersonality to its most extreme proportions, you will often find a hilarious caricature. You might find a "blob" or a "lapdog" or a "Poor Pitiful Pearl". You may want to act it out, write it out, or have it talk out loud and tell you what it needs. Then you can find out how to get these needs satisfied in more productive ways. Exaggerate it so much that it begins to amuse you.

- **You can count your blessings and see your attributes from a centered place, and you can emphasize alive and worthy parts of self.**

Trite as it may seem, it is something we often forget to do—as we go about bemoaning our difficulties and dragging our crosses around. When you begin to enumerate the areas of good fortune you have, your perspective changes. You can write it out if you like. Paul had always told himself he couldn't get ahead financially. Then he wrote about his "blessings": "I may not have much in the bank right now, but I'm living at a higher standard than ever before. I have a spacious two bedroom apartment with a garden area. I bought a brand new van for my work. I have health insurance, maintain a tax attorney, and I have an accountant (plus a tailor, masseur and a hypno-therapist). The money wad gets stretched a little thin sometimes, but I always make more." He was now able to see his fortune from another perspective.

- **You can realize that just because you didn't receive all the love you need does not mean you aren't worthy of it.**

It's quite natural to blame yourself if you haven't received unconditional (or even conditional) love. You wonder if you're worthy or if you did something to alienate the ones who were supposed to love you. "I must be bad "is a typical attitude. This point of view matures when you experience the inner workings of the people in your life. You see that often they've had unloving life experiences, and some have even had horrendous life experiences. This helps you to become more objective and to avoid self-blame. Often it's even possible to feel compassion for those who've been less than loving. Always it's possible to see yourself as worthy of love—even if it was not forthcoming from others.

• **You can watch the nature of your thoughts to give you more objectivity.**

Watching thoughts helps you to realize that you have thoughts, but you are not your thoughts, which change from moment to moment. This can help you to identify with your essential nature and not with your thoughts, which may be angry, sad, resentful, critical or depressed. You are much more than these changing states of mind.

• **You can center yourself in your essence to see your true inner worth.**

And that's what this book is about.

"A fear is a negative thought projected onto the future.
You might just as well think thoughts of transformation,
elevation, upliftment, and possibility. Fear is a
teacher, just as every feeling is, and most often,
the lesson is faith."

SamuEl

Healing Intimidation at Work

Karen had a rageful, abusive supervisor at work named Doris. Doris stood over her and watched her work and pointed out errors. She blamed Karen for every glitch in their project. When Karen asked her a question, Doris would give her an answer like, "Well, I'm not going to write it down for you!" Karen said she must have gone to the "Attila the Hun School of Management", and even though Karen had a wry sense of humor, she was suffering terribly at work.

I asked Karen to get a picture in hypnosis of something that related to her problems with Doris. She saw a picture of her Aunt Lucille, an angry and domineering aunt. Karen was ten, and she had just come to live with Aunt Lucille. This aging aunt was sitting by the window, and she said to Karen, "You have to earn your second class girl scout badge all over again. I don't care if you already have yours. You have to do what all the other girls are doing. So just get busy." The little girl had already done all the work and earned her badge; she felt controlled and intimidated but didn't speak up. The adult Karen, experiencing her strength, said to her aunt in trance, "Aunt Lucille, I've already earned my badge, and I don't have to work on it anymore." She was filled with a sense of power.

I asked Karen to see what might have been inside Aunt Lucille's mind. Miserably unhappy, this lonely woman had to raise a child all by herself when her husband went to the army and died on the battlefront. The child died as well, and Aunt Lucille grew very ill. She became embittered and mean-spirited, and Karen bore the brunt of the fallout.

In another session, Karen experienced Doris as a little girl. Her parents were hurting her, and she was sobbing. Karen felt a tender feeling in her heart for Doris, and she said to her, "I just want you to know that even though I care about how you feel, I already earned my second class badge. Now let's do this project together."

Another time, Karen saw herself as an eleven year old, and she was being taunted in the schoolyard for being "different". Two other girls were telling how they didn't like her and thought she was a terrible girl. Karen was shocked and hurt. Now, she saw herself on Mount Tamalpais wearing brightly colored clothes, and she was dancing with beautiful grace. The grown-up Karen danced with the girl on the mountain, both of them dancing in light, healing the schoolyard wounds.

She went to a past life experience in seventeenth century Ireland. She was a young girl with a black horse, and she was riding in the forest. She went into a clearing where she met up with several horrible men who terrified her. They killed her horse, raped her, cut off her legs, and then they killed her. Karen buried the girl by throwing her ashes in the ocean; she experienced a feeling of freedom, a liberation from an old deep pain. She then experienced a turquoise that emerged from her heart.

Standing Up

Karen is actually a powerful woman, but she had been carrying the visage of her aunt inside of her for years. She really did love Aunt Lucille and found her charming; she was also squashed by this old woman's tyranny. The most troubling part of her relationship with Aunt Lucille was the rage Karen felt for not having spoken up for herself.

She said, "I used to feel that if I expressed my power, I'd get killed for it." (Isn't that the root of most intimidation?) "Maybe I was right when I was a kid; I needed my parents and Aunt Lucille to be powerful in order to be safe in the world. If they were wrong, nobody would be there to take care of me. I feel more free now to express my power; I'm not operating as that ten year old girl anymore."

When Karen made the decision to come to terms with this problem, she had taken the first step. She said that doors to herself had been closed, and she hadn't even seen the doors in the first place. She was carrying around a heavy feeling for years, and she hadn't even known what it was. Karen's suffering propelled her to seek the roots. She found the doors and opened them.

Her healing came when she saw the significance of the girl scout badge. To her at the time, it was humiliating; though a small incident, it was symbolic of creativity and youth and a voice being crushed. Karen was able to regain her voice by first going to this early incident of suppression and then standing up to it.

She began to gain compassion by seeing Aunt Lucille as a being who was also suffering, who was working through her own issues in this life. This compassion gave her distance, cutting off the attachment Karen had felt to the intimidation. She again experienced compassion—this time for Doris, and she completed the cycle when she gently and firmly refused to cower in response to her demands.

Karen saw herself as a girl of eleven. This had been a hard year for her. Not only had she been tormented by her peers, but she had also been molested by her grandfather. (This was another issue that Karen was healing. She hadn't thought about this for years, but in hypnosis it came up emphatically for her, and she was more than willing to begin to handle it.) The experience of the girl dancing, wearing beautifully colorful clothes, was one of freedom and of self-expression.

The past-life experience in which her legs were cut off and in which she was then killed had profound meaning for Karen. All her life (this life), her legs had bothered her in one way or another. She also never felt fully grounded. She said. "Now I feel my legs. They're something that can 'carry me through'." She also felt that her legs had to do with trust, making her feel more safe in the world. It was significant to her that the girl have a "proper" burial and cremation. Karen had been victimized, but her spirit had been rescued. This gave her a sense of sanctity, respect, and trust. The turquoise that emerged from her heart was a symbol for her of strength.

Karen said, "The voice I can have to defend myself is not something I've been allowed to have. It's gotten lost, and in not being able to have the voice, what I felt instead was rage, enraged at being helpless. I found a voice that showed me I wasn't powerless, that people needed me as much as I needed them. It got rid of the rage and became a balancer, an equalizer."

She began to find humor in her daily life with Doris. She began to see her as "unconscious", as "interesting", as someone to watch. She became a witness and an adult with her.

Later Karen remembered a movie she saw when she was a child, about a girl named Esther:

"Esther was a little girl in Europe who went exploring with some boys. It was right after World War II, and they found a hand grenade. Her mother came looking for her, and the hand grenade exploded. Her friends and her mother were killed, and she was left blind and deaf-mute. And then she got adopted by a couple in the US, and she grew up as a poster child for the orphans of Europe. Then somehow both foster parents died, and she saw them die, and as she watched, she got her hearing, her eyesight, and her voice back. And in the last scene, people were going to hear her 'pathetic story'—but she was not pathetic anymore. She was a woman now, and she said, 'How can I explain to them what happened?' So she went in and told the truth.

"I feel like her, like I've never really been blind, deaf, and mute, but that's how I had to present myself to the world. Now I've got my eyesight back—and my hearing, and my voice." Karen appeared softened; all of her muscles had relaxed.

The Healing Principles

- **You can find keys to understanding current intimidating relationships in earlier wounds.**

    Look within at old wounds, and no doubt you will find the sources of your present vulnerabilities. There is often hurt, disappointment, and unfulfilled needs from earlier years. You can begin to come to terms with them and then set to work on fulfilling your needs with the healing force that is available to you in the present.

- **You can discover your personal power on an inner level because you have it within your essence, and you can heal the earlier wounds from this deep place.**

    It is a fact in everyone's life experience that we are always recreating the old wounds of childhood in order to finally heal them. That is why there is so much repetition of patterns in our lives. Making the connection with essence gives the opportunity to do things differently than you've ever done them before.

The experience of essence brings the experience of inner power.

- You can penetrate the psyche of your intimidator and often find weakness at the root of his or her behavior which can help you to feel more compassion and less fear.

    Usually it is the child or the undervalued part of the self that is capable of being intimidated. Understanding the motivations behind the perpetrator's actions can bring you into a place of greater maturity so that you can re-balance your vision of any situation.

Some Healing Stories

*"Within the human heart dwells a
shimmering effulgence whose brilliance surpasses even
that of the sun...Supreme joy blazes inside."*

Swami Muktananda

Healing Loneliness

Steve had a decent life—work that he enjoyed and a solid relationship—but inside he felt an abiding sense of loneliness. He couldn't quite put his finger on the causes, until he began to go in trance to some of his earliest life experiences.

I asked him in hypnosis to go back and see any picture that related to his loneliness. He saw himself as three years old in his high chair. No one seemed to know he was there. Because he was a quiet boy, he didn't call attention to himself by acting up, and it felt as if he were all alone, even though the whole family was around the table with him.

Steve looked carefully at his mother to see why she didn't attend to the boy more. She was carrying a heavy burden—the care of five children—and her body looked heavy as if it were made of lead. I suggested that he look at what she might have been like as a child herself. Steve saw her as a little girl sitting on the steps of her house all alone. No one was paying any attention to her either, and he could feel her alienation and her pain.

Steve took the little boy out of his high chair and brought him to a stream in the woods. They walked along the stream for a while, together looking at all the wildflowers and rocks and the ripples on the water. As they waded into the stream together, the water gradually covered their bodies. This was healing water that washed over them, and it washed away the hurt and the pain of loneliness and neglect. Steve picked up the little boy and held him closely, telling him that he'd never have to feel so alone again.

In another session, Steve saw himself as a boy of fifteen, living on his farm in the Midwest. He had so many chores to do that he had no time to be a teen. He wondered why he had so few friends and no girlfriend. He felt isolated and forlorn. I suggested that he might like to create some companionship for the boy. A "girlfriend" appeared before him, and she became his companion, as the two of them talked, held hands, did the chores, went to the movies, and laughed with one another.

I told him, "You're not that lonely little boy anymore. Now that you're grown, you've come to know the source of love within you that you can bring to all the isolated and alienated parts of yourself."

Lonely Roots Run Deep

Steve's loneliness began long ago, not only from the early neglect of an overburdened parent—but from the psyche of that parent as well. He was able to see his mother's own alienation by "opting in"—by exploring her psyche while he was in a deeply relaxed state. He had never realized how difficult it had been for her to raise five children. It was no wonder that he was alone in a room full of people. They were all so distracted, they had no awareness of his presence.

Being able to see his mother as a child also gave Steve an expanded perspective. He had never imagined that she was quite so lonely and desolate as she had been as a child. Seeing this gave him compassion for her and showed him how the pattern was being perpetuated in him.

The healing water elementally washed away the hurt. This, of course, doesn't mean that all the hurt is gone forever, but it is a symbolic washing.

Steve is able to bring companionship not only to the little boy, but to the lonely teenager. He brings this healing bond from the part of himself that is already strong and connected and loving.

The Healing Principles

- **You can see into another's psyche and increase your compassion.**

    You have the ability to see into the minds of others, to assess their motivations, find the causes of their behavior. This is not done to justify their behavior, but to help you understand it, become more objective, and ultimately more free.

- **You can observe the early experiences of another to get greater understanding of current behavior.**

    Not only is it helpful to explore your own early experiences—but it can be a healing experience for you to see into the histories of the other people in your life.

- **You can bring companionship to alienated parts of the self from the strong and loving essence.**

    There is always within you a part that is whole, a part that knows how to be a true companion. This is the part of you that is already healed and that brings wholeness to everything it touches.

"*Whenever your mind begins to worry, agonize,
project, or bemoan its fate, you can say,
'I am healing myself now.'
This marshals the forces of healing within you.*"

SamuEl

Healing Sexual Abuse

Sarah had been abused by everyone in her family. She felt an eerie sense of doom and a paralyzing fear whenever she thought about her childhood. As a girl, she had been raped and beaten by her father; she had also been verbally abused and humiliated by her mother and all her brothers and sisters. She was the youngest child in her family and the family scapegoat.

She knew that she wanted to recover, but the memories were too painful to recall. How could she go back there? I suggested to her that she could go back into her past little by little. She could create a feeling of safety for herself before confronting the most difficult parts of her past. I suggested that she begin by imagining in trance that she was throwing a blanket of protective light over all her childhood memories to make them safe to remember.

Feeling safe now, she decided that it was okay to do some more exploration in trance. Having a rich imagination, she found herself in a castle. She opened a door, and before her she saw a gorgeous display of multi-colored jars. Picking up the ruby red jar, she drank it, sensing it was a special remedy for her blood. As she drank the blue one, it calmed her heart, and the clear one cleansed her system. She was beginning to heal her physical body first.

Now she felt more courageous, and she opened herself to experiencing the old and terrible wounds. The first image she saw was of herself as a small girl lying on the floor in bandages, and she protected both herself and the girl with healing light.

I asked her if she were ready to go back to her childhood environment. She went back to a garage where she had been attacked by her father; it brought up a feeling of rage in her. She said, "I have to destroy this room." She chose to bomb it from above, and it made a large hole in the earth. Images of healing came up next, as she filled the hole with new earth; next she planted a rain forest there—complete with exotic parrots and trees. Again she covered the young girl with protective healing light.

More visions came. Her psyche was opening up to reveal more and more information. She was hiding in a laundry bin, curled up in the fetal position. Her father was on a rampage, and she had found a good place to hide; she knew he'd never look for her in the laundry bin. I suggested that she could rescue the child. In trance, Sarah took the little girl out of the bin and brought her to a tree in the yard where they both climbed up into the treehouse far away from harm. The two of them, adult and child, sat huddled together, both of them comforted.

In another trance session, she was a little girl, very sick with the measles. Something was terrifying her; she screamed piercingly. There was a monster there with large yellow eyes peering down on her. Again, she reached into her arsenal and took out a fire bomb and blasted the monster. This time, she asked to be covered with silver light.

Back in the apothecary room, she saw another red bottle—beautiful and hot and dangerous. This time the bottle was filled with the fire of fury. As she drank it, she felt a fire within her. The fire was now her power. She was really able now to get in touch with the fury that she had held inside. I suggested that she not only feel the fire as anger, but also as a powerful energy of creativity. Then I suggested that she experience it as a healing that comes in the form of light.

Another time, she saw herself as four years old, standing there with no clothes on after her father had beaten her. She threw her toys at her father until she was exhausted, and then she went into a mountain stream to cleanse and wash away the terrible feelings. She felt the healing water all over her body as it washed away the fear and the rage, and then a sunbeam dried her off and soothed her.

In another picture, she was now ten, dressed in red sandals and a green dress, and she was lying on the ground, desolate and devastated. Her dress was raised up, and she was saying, "My daddy...." In trance, she brought in the adult Sarah to rescue this devastated child. She wrapped her in a blanket, washed her and gave her some special healing remedies. She held her and loved her and took her home.

In trance, she began to speak out loud to her father, telling him how his rage had left lifelong scars on her, but that now she is in touch with another force within her, her own power to heal.

The Healing Power of Her Essence

At first Sarah had been too fearful to even look at her childhood, especially at her father's sexual abuse. Gradually, she began to feel safer as she created "protection" by putting healing light around her entire childhood. Soon the powerful and imaginative parts of her began to emerge as the images became more specific and graphic. When she saw the apothecary jars, her outer behavior changed as the imagined medicines soothed her. She felt more safe and protected; she became less irritable and more calm. She said, "I don't feel like the past is creeping into the present so much anymore." She was paving the way to go more deeply.

When she "bombed" the garage, the improvements became even more noticeable. She realized that there is a power of the present that can heal the events of the past. As she continually covered the young girl with healing light, she was actually creating healing experiences that were now a part of her "history."

She developed more courage to experience events of the past. She was coming closer to her essence as a powerful being. This "power of the present" gave her fuel. And although many of her own healing choices were to destroy (by bombing, for example), others were tender and gentle. She almost playfully brought the young girl to a treehouse for protection. Another time, she wrapped her in a blanket and washed her. Going to the healing water was another act of tenderness. Finding her own essence helped her to find sources of both power and love.

This is how she was able to develop a healing consciousness. She could call upon this healing power inside of her to make the wounded parts whole. She could confront and mend these ancient traumas that had been incapacitating her for years. One time, she remarked, "I didn't realize that I had been walking around in shock all this time."

At one point, an old familiar pain, similar to menstrual pain, had come up in her body, and as she became aware of it, the pain disappeared. She had recognized its origins in this event that had happened when she was just a girl of ten. She began to cry, releasing the old wounds.

She noticed discernable changes in her life. One day, she said, "I've been more lighthearted. I feel like a burden has been lifted. I've had a massive sense of release. I haven't felt as furious. When I saw the desperate tired person behind the anger, it helped me. When I was getting angry, I stood back and said, 'This fury has been hurting me; I don't have to let it hurt me anymore.' I've been fatigued all my life, and my energy is coming back. My shame is gone; I realize that I wasn't bad and I didn't do it. I feel so much more calm."

She had been able to develop more witness consciousness and more wisdom—and this opened up new areas for her in being able to come to terms with the terror and anger that had been controlling her life for years.

The Healing Principles

• **You can overcome your fear of dealing with the past.**

Not everyone is afraid of "going back there"—but you may be. The traumas may have been so great, that you are still terrorized by them. If you have a desire to heal, you can overcome the fear by going slowly, by creating safety, and by remembering the power and love of your essence that can help you do your healing work.

• **You can bring more love into your "history".**

Your love can reach back into your past to "re-paint" it, and you can actually change your brain's imprinting about past events. When you give love and attention to yourself as a child, for example, you may be able to experience actual changes in old feelings of alienation that you've been carrying around.

• **You can empower yourself to stand up to those who abuse you.**

It is possible in trance to experience your own ability to assert yourself, and then you can create the actual experience in your life. You find out how to do it by tapping into your own essential power while in trance where you can then "rehearse" its actual expression. (See more on "Trance Rehearsal").

- **You can experience and transmute your anger.**

    You need not keep your anger inside to let it fester and turn into depression and lack of self-love. You can experience it in imagery or in your body or in sounds. There is an alchemy to anger: *fire* becomes *fuel for action* becomes the *light of healing.* The heat of your fury can ignite your creative forces. You can then experience this energy as the force of light.

- **You can confront your "monsters".**

    You can look a monster in the eye and say, "If you think you're going to scare me, you're wrong!" Fairy tales and myths describe the archetypal journeys of souls going through the dark forest of their lives on their quest for whatever their holy grail might be (relationships, empowerment, enlightenment). The challenges or the monsters they meet up with serve to strengthen these souls. Your "monster" may be a repetitive thought or fear, and it's inspiring to realize that you can stare it down and let it know that it can't have power over you anymore.

- **You can observe your own spontaneous imagery and let it show you what's deep inside.**

    On the screen of your mind, watch your own pictures, and observe what's going on in your psyche. Because in trance you have a heightened awareness, you can often see interrelationships between events and their causes, and you can access information that may have been hidden from you.

- **You can heal with light and water and with the experience of witness consciousness.**

    See "How It's Done" for a more complete explanation of the significance of these experiences.

More
Healing
Stories

These stories, as well as the preceding ones, are parts of ongoing healing programs for each individual. The stories are included here to show you some possibilities available for healing specific issues; they are intended to be included in more extensive healing programs. They serve to point out healing potentials for everyone.

Healing A Career Problem

For years, Steve had been a carpenter—but that's not really what he wanted to do. He was a skilled people-worker; he knew how to work with people to help them grow and change. But Steve at age 31 was still making his living with his hammer and saw, and he wondered when he'd be able to fully do the work as a counselor and teacher that he really wanted to do. He came to hypnotherapy because he suspected there was something inside of him that was holding him back.

He relaxed very deeply, and I asked him what was the first thing that he either thought of or felt that related to his delay in doing his true work. The first word that came to him was "fear".

"Where is it in your body?" I asked.

"It's at the pit of my stomach." he answered.

"When did you first feel that feeling? Do you have a picture of that time in your mind?" I questioned him.

"It's my birth," he replied, tears streaming down his cheeks. His birth had been traumatic. His mother spent many hours in labor, and he almost didn't make it into this world. I asked him if he'd like to heal this picture of his birth.

In this new picture, he was not only the infant, but he was the doctor as well. He brought the baby out with great love. He dimmed the lights in the room, put on soft music, and, gently and with the greatest love, he stroked the baby's body—its tiny arms and legs and back. Then he put the baby on his mother's body to nurse. All the while, he was experiencing this profound love as the baby, and yet he was also the loving adult. He wept with joy.

The next picture he saw was of himself as a boy of four. His parents were fighting, and they sent him and his sister out of the house. Again he felt this fear at the pit of his stomach. His parents were engaged in a merciless brawl, and he was sick inside. He again brought his adult self in to heal and comfort the boy. They went walking together to get as far away from that house as they could. He carried the boy through the streets, stroking his back and hugging him. There was healing light around both of them.

I then reminded him: "You're not that little boy anymore. You're grown now, and this fear is not yours anymore. Soon you will be able to do your true work, as you wash away all this fear from your childhood years." Steve emerged from trance radiant and cleansed, and after some more inner work, he soon began his path as a counselor and teacher.

Healing a Comfort Habit

Janice had been biting her lip since she was a little girl, sometimes so severely that her mouth would be raw and her teeth worn down. When she was small, her parents had stopped her from sucking her thumb, and Janice realized that biting her lip was a way of being able to suck on something that they might not notice. When Janice went back in hypnosis and visited her inner child, she began to weep profusely when she realized how abandoned this little girl felt. She was able to give love and attention to her inner child, and she realized that biting her lip had always been a great comfort for her. She received the posthypnotic suggestion that instead of biting her lip, now she could stroke her own cheek, and this would give her the same gratification. The first day after her session, she stayed in bed and mourned the loss of her habit. After that, the habit vanished, and she didn't even need to stroke her face in order to stop. The contact with her inner child and the realization of the role this comfort habit had played for her had given her the freedom to end this habit that had been with her for so many years.

Healing a Sexual Problem

Bob had an intermittant impotence problem. At times, he enjoyed his sexuality. At other times, he'd lose his erection. I asked him to go inside and to look at what his thoughts were just before making love. The first was a picure of his father standing there and judging him. His father was Victorian in his morality and very critical of Bob. The next series of thoughts were Bob's own "failure thoughts": "You'll never keep it up. You've had trouble before. It's already drooping."

I reminded him that his father, being human, had sexual relations himself. I asked Bob to imagine his father's sexuality. This served to humanize his father, and now, feeling his power, Bob was able to stare at his father with "laser eyes" and dissolve him in his mind. He then remembered some of his prime sexual experiences and created, instead of failure thoughts, a repertoire of success. After that, making love was easy and great.

Bob had a sense of humor also. When I asked him to find his inner guidance, two wise admonitions came through: "Always wear seat belts...and never wear blue shoes with a brown suit."

Healing a Prosperity Problem

Lois never had enough money. She was competent and able, but she had trouble paying her bills. I asked her to see who was the person inside who had so much trouble with money. She saw a raggedy young girl who looked forlorn. Her head was bowed, and her mind was saying, "Nothing can ever come to any good." She called her "Poor Pitiful Pearl", the name of a doll dressed as a waif she had seen as a child . This is how Lois felt about herself inside. There was also another part of Lois, a strong, clear-minded woman who knew her life's direction. I asked her to get in touch with this part by making contact with her essence. This part of her went to the raggedy one and asked her to look at the strong one's goals. She showed her what she wanted to do in life, what her aspirations and her goals were, and she enlisted her co-operation. She said to "Pearl", "I need your help in my success. I realize you feel forlorn and poor, but there is so much I want to do in life, and I need your support." She hugged raggedy Pearl, and the two of them merged to form one abundant, competent, self-actualizing woman.

Healing Powerlessness in Relationship

Mark was married to someone who was outspoken and strong; in contrast, Mark felt destined to "doormathood" because he sometimes kept silent instead of speaking up, and he had no sense of his own power. I asked him in hypnosis to find an image of his power.

He saw himself with a sword, in a fencing stance. " I'm cutting through b.s.," he said. His wife had her own sword, but it felt good to Mark because he was standing his ground. His sword was his potency; it wasn't a symbol of violence. It was an opportunity to "make love, not war." He felt his own boldness. I asked him to describe the fencer. "He's not fearless," Mark said. "He feels fear and goes right to the heart of it with his sword. It's exhilarating. He also stands up in front of people and performs. He loves himself. People aren't attacked by him. They're empowered by him. He's not macho; the point isn't that he's great. He shows you that you can be powerful too—powerful in a real way, going to the heart of things. " He saw himself and his wife now laughing and embracing. The power balance now began to shift in Mark's relationship with his wife.

Healing Anger in Relationship

Ruth was furious at a friend who she felt had betrayed her. I asked her if she'd like to experience her anger in hypnotherapy. She was ready and eager, for the rage was overwhelming to her. In hypnosis, she saw herself slashing her friend with a knife—all the way down her body. She slashed with fury, and she cut her friend wide open. Out of the wound came a "light body companion", a friend made of light, who was soft and loving. She came to Ruth and embraced her. Ruth had been able to go to the other side of her anger, to turn the fire into light by allowing the anger to run its course. Soon she was able to stand back and see her relationship with her friend more clearly and allow the love of their friendship to re-emerge.

" The light of the universe is a real phenomenon.
It is an emanation from the universe and from all
living things. It creates harmony and heals, and
when you feel this light, it is as if you
are being showered with grace.
It uplifts all your cells to a radiant state."

SamuEl

Self-Healing:

What You Can Do On Your Own

For deep inner work, it helps to have a guide, a teacher, a hypnotherapist, or a wise friend. The inner terrain can be challenging, and a guide can help you to move more skillfully on these trails. But you can do a great deal of healing work on your own.

Help Your Mind: Watch Your Thoughts

Stand back and become the witness of your thoughts and subpersonalities. Become aware of the kinds of thoughts you habitually think. Do you tend to catastrophize, to create the Worst Possible Scenario for the events of your life? (This is also called the"Vay Is Mir" or"Woe is Me" syndrome, where everything is a potential disaster for you.). Do you tend to think depressive thoughts, to feel that you won't be able to be happy? Do you think anxiety thoughts, creating all kinds of dangers for yourself, most of them in your lively imagination? Do you tend to obsess, to keep going over and over certain thoughts? Watch also how your subpersonalities are taking control in certain situations as "Poor Me" or "Not Okay" or "Have to Be Perfect to Be Loved".

When you stand back and observe, you begin to get some degree of objectivity. You may want to record your findings in a journal. Or you may want to use a tape recorder to dialog with these thoughts or subpersonalities.

You might want to exaggerate the tendencies so much that they become caricatures, even to the point of becoming humorous. You might want to bring your essence in to remind your subpersonalities that you do have innate worth or that you are doing competent work or that you are healing yourself now.

It works to affirm who you really are, to tell the truth to all other inner influences, to remind them over and over again:

> "I am the power of healing, and within me is
> love. I am strong and whole, and I am healing
> myself now!"

Using the words "I am" to begin your affirmation helps bring your essence in to help with any situation. If you are going through a particularly difficult time, such as a time of anxiety or depression, you can watch the thoughts that come up, and every time they do, you can say, "No, that's not so. I am healing myself now." (See more affirmations on a special page that follows.)

You may also want to enlist the support of a recalcitrant subpersonality by showing it your goals; you can take the more dysfunctional part and show it what you really want to do in life, and you can ask for its assistance. You may want to give a subpersonality some other way of getting its needs met so that it won't sabotage you any longer; so for example, if a part of you is eating too much in order to handle certain thoughts or to get some comfort, you may want to find other ways that can help to quiet your mind or bring comfort. You may also want to merge your subpersonality with essence so that you will be free to act from a more centered place.

Being able to watch yourself more objectively can help to free you from the bondage of repetitive thoughts or from stubborn subpersonalities. When you get in touch with your essence by relaxing and centering yourself, you have greater ability to be objective and to bring your strength, wisdom, and love in to heal your situation.

Exercise: Write or use your tape recorder to identify your specific dominant difficult thoughts and subpersonalities. Exaggerate and experience them, and then find ways of helping them.

Induce Trance

There are many techniques for deep relaxation or self-hypnosis. I'll elaborate on two of them here. Other ideas are in the section called "How It's Done".

For self-hypnosis, first find a comfortable place where you won't be interrupted. You can either sit or lie down. Close your eyes, and take a deep breath in. Breathe in and out three times, and begin counting from thirty down to one. As you count, relax various parts of your body. You can say, "My feet are relaxing. My hands are relaxing."—and so on, as you count. This will focus your mind inward and help you to experience a deeply relaxed state. When you feel relaxed, you can then do posthypnotic suggestions, affirmations, visualizations, and any of the other techniques I'm describing here.

Here is a more extended trance induction that you can use, either by having someone read it to you or by taping it and listening to your own voice:

"Just relax and get comfortable now, and take a deep breath in and exhale. Just let go of any stress or tension. Take another deep breath in, and exhale once again. Let a peaceful wave of energy wash over your body and your mind. Take one more deep breath in and exhale once again, and go deeper and deeper now into a wonderful state of relaxing peace. You feel very comfortable now, very relaxed. Your body is becoming so relaxed that you don't even want to move. You are releasing and relaxing, drifting down deeper and deeper. It's like drifting off to sleep; yet you remain aware. As I count from five to one, you go even more deeply. Five: Feel yourself sinking deeper and deeper into a state of relaxation, further and further away from all outside concerns. Four: Each number carries you deeper, drifting down deeper and deeper. Three: Going so

deeply that every part of your body relaxes. Your mind relaxes. Nothing else concerns you at all. On the next count, you feel how much more deeply relaxed you are. One: Deep, deeply relaxed.

These feelings of relaxation bring you greater and greater comfort, as you feel yourself relaxing, going deeper and deeper. You feel as if you are surrounded by a blanket of peace. Your body is relaxing with wonderful feelings of pleasant heaviness. You feel so comfortable, going deeper and deeper within."

Make Your Own Hypnosis Tapes

You need one or two tape recorders, the first one to record on, and the second, for music, if you'd like it as a background. Choose some soft and relaxing music. Prepare a relaxation or induction. (See the tape transcripts on the following pages for specific wording.) You can write out your own script for the tapes, or you can use the material from this book. If you write your own script, include the issues that are important for you. State all the issues in an affirmative way; for example, "I am able to feel more and more love for myself and to be easier on myself." You can address yourself as "you" or "I", whichever you prefer. And keep your suggestions in the present. For example, "I am a talented pianist." is preferable to "I will be a talented pianist."

Begin the tape with a deep relaxation, and then continue to inspire and affirm all good for yourself. Again, check the sample scripts for ideas. Remember at the end to conclude the trance. "I'm going to count from one to five and when I do, I will come back to waking consciousness feeling full of life, energy and well-being."—or whatever you would like to say.

These tapes can be extraordinarily helpful for you

and for others. If you listen to them on a regular basis, they can support the transformational healing work you are doing. They can give you a cushion of healing, comfort, and reinforcement. Here's an example of a tape format:

How to Make a Tape for Loving Yourself as a Child

After you do your hypnotic induction, you can include in your tape some special ingredients:

- Walk down some stairs and through a door, and see a place from your childhood. See yourself as a child—at any age.

- Observe yourself as a child for a while, and experience what you are thinking and feeling.

- Bring yourself into the scene at the age you are now, and give the child support and love. Perhaps you'll see yourself with your arm around the child, or you may want to hold the child. You may want to let him or her know how you feel about being there—and you may want to reassure the child that you'll always be available, especially if the child feels lonely or abandoned.

- You may want to play with the child, go to some of the wondrous places you loved or play some of your favorite games.

- This can create a reunification of parts of yourself—where you can become your own parent and bring love and kindness and compassion to the child within you.

Experience Your Own Inner Imagery in Self-Hypnosis

If you'd like to do self-hypnosis without making a tape for yourself, there are several techniques you can use. One of these is to make suggestions to yourself after you've become relaxed. The other is to freely explore your inner imagery and create self-healing experiences.

If you want to explore your inner imagery, first relax. Then ask your inner mind to show you any images that pertain to a specific or a general topic that you've chosen to look at. Let images come spontaneously to your inner eye. Without judging or changing, just let yourself view your own pictures. If you would like, you can then bring in healing images—healing water or light, love and care for your child within and for yourself now, experiences of parents as they were in childhood—or any healing experience that is meaningful for you.

You can ask to see what images are linked to a specific issue, such as those that are connected with your fear of heights or your aversion to spiders—and these images might take you to early childhood experiences and even to past lives.

You can also do posthypnotic suggestion by saying affirmations to yourself while you're deeply relaxed. You'll find some general affirmations on the following pages, or you can make up your own.

You might want to have a guide or hypnotherapist for this type of work; however, if you feel ready, you can do it on your own.

Write

If you'd like to get in touch with your inner guidance, you can do hypnotic writing. You may have a specific life question, or you may simply want to get in touch with your guidance. Have a paper and pencil ready.

First relax deeply by inducing a trance state. This can be mild, medium, or deep. As you are relaxing, tell yourself, "I am now becoming a vehicle for wisdom and guidance to come through me. I am a hollow bamboo through which I receive guidance. I am opening to receive any information that my higher self would like to bring through me. I am a channel for wisdom and guidance." Then open your eyes, but remain very relaxed. Take your pencil in your hand, and begin to write. You may want to write a question, or you may simply begin writing and let your higher self decide what topic to address.

If nothing comes to you, open up the flow of words by writing anything, even if at first it sounds like nonsense. Re-affirm that you are bringing forth wisdom and guidance, and you will no doubt find that something of value ultimately comes through you. It might help you to have a trigger device. One of these is to ask the name of your guide and then write your guide's name at the top of your paper. To get this name, just close your eyes, ask for the name, and take the first name that comes to your mind. Another trigger device is to begin writing a letter to yourself ("Dear....") and know that this letter is from your inner guidance.

As you write, stay relaxed, and just let the words flow as easily as possible. You may receive very specific information ("You are to leave your job next month and move to Arizona.") or it may be very general

("You are on the right path. Keep up the good work.")

You will be amazed at the quality of guidance and information that you can receive from this process. Trust that you can have access to your own channels of wisdom, and allow it to come through you whenever you'd like to experience your own truth.

Meditate

It is always helpful to quiet yourself and to sit and meditate. The main difference between meditation and self-hypnosis is that in meditation, you quiet your mind enough to be responsive to your essence, and you simply allow it to come through you. In self hypnosis you may do visualizations or affirmations, or you may create posthypnotic suggestions; still the experience of relaxation and of essence is the same.

One way of meditating is to find a comfortable place to be, a place where you won't be disturbed. If you like, you can use a mantra. The one I like is the "Ham Sa" mantra, (pronounced "Hum Sah"). You say "Ham" to yourself as you breathe in, and you say "Sa" as you exhale. You keep your focus on the mantra as you breathe naturally. If thoughts come to you, just let them come, and then let them go, like birds flying across the sky. You can meditate for as long as you like to, anywhere from ten minutes to one hour. Meditation is a beautiful way to experience your essence.

Breathe

During the course of your day, focus your awareness on your breathing. If you feel anxiety or anger or tension, your breathing will be high up in your chest, and the breaths will be shallow and rapid. As you notice this, you will be able to slow down your breathing; then you can breathe in and out very deeply. This will help to transform the emotions and experiences you are going through. A good exercise to help your breathing is to breathe rhythmically. Breathe in for six counts; then hold for six. Breathe out for six, and hold for six again. Breathe deeply, and you will find an amazing change in the way you're feeling and behaving.

Exercises

1. Visualize yourself as a child, at any age that your inner mind would like to show you. Go inside and bring love to this child.

2. Find a subpersonality that you often experience as a part of your behavior. Look at some of your responses or inner dialogue. Exaggerate this subpersonality and act it out—either on paper or verbally. See how you might give this subpersonality what it needs in a new way, a creative instead of a destructive new behavior.

3. Imagine healing yourself with light or water. You can use the Ball of Light visualization or the light and water healings as explained in the "How It's Done" section.

4. Keep a log of your most predominant thoughts. If you find them consistently negative, see how you might speak to these thoughts. Tell them that their self-defeating approach is not the only alternative, and show them new ways of perceiving by offering realities that are more life-affirming. (See "Healing Feelings of Unworthiness" for more examples).

5. Find a symbol of your essence that feels comfortable to you, and focus on it throughout the day. This symbol might have to do with music, gems, water, light, great beings, or whatever your creative imagination brings through you. In trance, you may be able to find this symbol by asking to have it shown to you while you are very relaxed.

6. Write down all the blessings that you've been given. Make a list of all the advantages you've had in life, all the good fortune, all the gifts you've been given. Remember, even the disadvantages might be in your favor. I've already spoken about the woman who thanked her parents for never being there when she really needed them, for it made her realize that all she really needed was herself.

7. Examine your parents, friends, siblings, children from a detached state, seeing them as human beings who are working out their problems and challenges just as you are working out yours. Look at their past, their paths, their predominant thought patterns and look at the possibility of maintaining some of that objectivity in your daily life with them.

8. Practice self-hypnosis by making a tape for yourself or by doing a trance induction.

9. Find a habit that you'd like to transform, and do it through self-hypnosis, posthypnotic suggestion, and your connection with your essence. You may want to make a tape for yourself, and you may want to include the following:

- Reasons for wanting to change (what you don't like about the habit)
- What you might do instead of the habit (for example, eating fruit instead of candy or doing deep breathing and self-hypnosis instead of smoking)
- How your life would improve with the habit gone
- Affirmative statements about your ability to change
- Visualizations of yourself without the habit
- Reminders from your essence of your real nature: strength, wisdom, and love.

10. Do a "trance rehearsal" for a life that is creative and fulfilling. See yourself as you'd like to look and feel and be. See as many details as possible, and accept that the transformation is happening in you now.

*"All things are working towards
the upliftment of this world in spite of its pain.
Have complete faith in the process."*

SamuEl

Affirmations

- I am learning and evolving.

- I am able to change the way I see my past, present, and future.

- I am healing my childhood.

- I am healing myself now.

- I am loved and healed.

- I am essence.

- I am love, and I am nurturing myself.

- I am more than the personalities and voices within me.

- I am centered in my essence.

- I am honoring my own inner worth.

- I am counting my blessings.

- I am observing my mind and my thoughts.

- I am powerful, loving, and wise.

- I am able to handle my own emotions.

- I am the healing power of the universe, and within me is all love.

"The purpose of our life, the purpose
of our incarnation within the human body, is to journey
back to the source....Many thousands of people around
the world, perhaps even hundreds of thousands, have
experienced that they are permeated by light, that they
receive answers from within."

Cris Griscom

Trance Narratives for Taping

Experiencing Your Essence

Just let yourself relax and get comfortable now, take a deep breath in, and exhale. Just let go of any stress or tension. Take another deep breath in, and exhale once again, and let a peaceful wave of energy wash over your body and your mind. Now take in one more deep breath, and exhale. Go deeper and deeper now, feeling very comfortable and peaceful, allowing your body and your mind to relax fully, totally, and completely. Just drift and float, further and further away from any external distractions, and go deeper and deeper within yourself to a peaceful place inside.

When you're this relaxed, you're able to quiet your everyday thoughts and to go to a place deep inside yourself, a very special place, deep within, that is your essence. It's in this place that you feel a sense of safety. It's in this place that you feel love. Let yourself just experience that safety and that love, almost as if a blanket were thrown around you, cushioning you; feel the love, deep inside of yourself. Get in touch with the love that's at the center of your being, molecules of love all through you, dancing and vibrating. This vibrating love is your essence. It's at your core. It's what you're made of. And at your core is also true wisdom and guidance. When you're in this experience, you're able to bring forth answers, understanding, knowing, from a place that's deep within you. When you relax and go to your inner being, you make contact with this sense of safety, a haven of safety within you from which you can experience love and guidance. This place within you is also pure consciousness, existence itself. There is no need to have any reason for existing, no need to know, no need to do; all you have to do is to be. It's a quality of being that is who you are deep within. And you're also the quality of doing, of creating. This is Shiva, pure awareness, and Shakti, the active, dancing creative part that is bringing forth into the world an expression of your energy. You can get in touch with your own source of safety, love, wisdom, awareness, creativity, and joy. This is a joy from deep inside yourself, a joy that doesn't depend on anything exterior to you. No one needs to make you happy or to make you laugh; you have an inner joy that you can feel from time to time when you're able to go within, a deep, profound reasonless joy that's the nature of your essence.

You have within you truth, love, wisdom, joy, and peace. This place within you is pure peace. There is no turmoil, there is no chaos, just peace in this inner sanctuary. There is creation and there is destruction, and at the core of that is peace. This is your essence. Great beings have called it Sat Chit Ananda, Satchitananda. Sat: truth; Chit: awareness; Ananda: love. Deep inside of you is where this resides. It's a kernal within your being, and when you reach into this place, you begin to solve the problems of your daily living , just by reaching in, just by going here because you remind yourself that this is who you are. Reminding yourself of this can help you to observe and to heal all the other parts of yourself that are operating in less functional ways. When you dive in, when you travel down deeply into this magnificent ocean within you, you're able to find the key, the center of yourself from which all healing radiates out. You can operate from this place in your life more and more, become this more and more as you bring your essence into manifestation.

You are that essence. You are born with that essence within you. When you die that essence remains. And as you dive deeply down into this extraordinary fountain within yourself, this resource—so great, so deep—you get in touch with the ways in which you experience essence on a daily basis—in beauty and love, the beauty of nature, the love of a friend, a child, and the wisdom that helps you to come to terms with any problem, in the joy you experience on a happy occasion, in the peace that you know after you've solved or settled something. When you relax, you can experience pure awareness, relaxed awareness that underlies your everyday mind. This experience can help you with your everyday mind that ceaslessly chatters about one thing or another: some of the thoughts, you learned as a child; some of the thoughts you brought with you from another lifetime; some of the thoughts, the tendencies of your mind, you've picked up along the way; some of the thoughts that have been your destiny to think. Now you can take your destiny and hold it more and more in the palm of your own hand when you reach in to this essence, for another one of the qualities of essence is power, strength, dynamic pure energy that is yours. And that is why you have within you radiance, greatness, beauty, and wonder. And that's why you can reach within to experience it. Just know that the more you do, the more you experience truth, peace, understanding and love in your life. It is very great to be able to reach in on a daily basis to this core, this resource, that lies within.

Tape for Being Easier on Yourself and Letting Go of Pain

You're on a quiet road now surrounded by trees. You walk up a tiny hill and through more trees until you're in a light and open area with grass and flowers. You're sitting by a small pond, and in the water you can see an ugly duckling. You realize that it represents your fear and anger and parts of yourself you don't like. As you sit there, you feel so much love for the duckling, so much love for that part of yourself you find hard to love. The more you love it, the more you are willing to see it in a new way. Your love and acceptance turns it into a beautiful swan.

The sky is clear and blue, and you feel warm and loving and relaxed. You let go, able to love yourself and others, listening to the sounds of the swan in the water, feeling the peace inside yourself, feeling a sense of deep self-love, self-acceptance knowing that in your essence, in your deepest inner core, you are whole, complete, secure, peaceful and good. And it's only the critical mind that can criticize something that is good. You feel a sense of compassion for yourself, of caring for yourself, realizing you're something far beyond what you could even imagine.

You're part of the universe with goodness inside of you and outside of you too, and as a part of the universe, you belong to everything, and everything is a part of you, and you take on an expanded view of your own self. And as you relax more and more deeply and feel better and better about yourself, you feel a sense of your own self-confidence building, knowing that you have abilities and talents—so many things that you're able to do in life, feeling confident about your talents, and realizing that the things you're able to do also help you to relax. You remember how you can feel really in touch with yourself. You feel a sense of self-love. You are in touch with your essence. And this self-love grows and grows inside of you until you feel warm and radiant. You have a special radiance inside of you that glows from within and sends love to every part of your body and your own mind. You are a person of real worth. You have so many abilities and potentials, and as you let go of self-criticism, anger, and fear, more and more you are able to feel a sense of peace, and more and more, any discomfort in your body just begins to dissolve. If there is any discomfort in your body, just find it now, and just imagine that there is a warm comforting hand in that place. It's just absorbing any of the discomfort just like a paper towel will absorb ink from a pen. This comforting warm hand is pulling away all of the discomfort. And as it pulls away the discomfort, you realize that you are able to be easier on yourself now. You are good, and you deserve to be treated with love, especially by your own self. And if you have any other discomfort, just imagine that a hand is there too. It pulls away the discomfort as if it were a magnet. You're able to relax so deeply, to feel a sense of grace, like the swan upon the water.

You know deep down inside that your mind can heal you. All you need to do is to engage your will and be determined to heal your own self, and you say to yourself the healing words: "With the wisdom of my higher self, and the power of my healing mind, I am healing myself now of the tendency to be hard on myself." And you see yourself as healed and you see a beautiful light around you, glowing, radiating, beautiful. And you can say this anytime you want, and if your mind is working overtime, you say to yourself, "I am healing myself now." And your thoughts become more and more quiet. You feel better and better now— every single day. All discomforts in your body are released. Relaxing as you relax every day; releasing as you release, every day. Letting go of thoughts and discomforts, of anything that does not give love to your own self. You become happier and happier every day. External events change as your internal events change, and the deeper parts of yourself hear these messages.

You are a being of the universe. The same molecules that are in you are in everything else. And you are made of love. That's who you are at your very essence.

And now, coming back to waking consciousness, feeling wonderful, feeling grounded and centered, energetic and alive and happy. 1-2-3-4-5.

"See the advantage in everything.
This can help you to have a happy life no matter
what the obstacles may be."

SamuEl

My
Story

You might be interested in knowing how I came to do this work. It has grown out of the work I have been doing on myself for many years.

Going deeply into the inner worlds started when I was a little girl. My favorite radio program was "Let's Pretend", and the world of the imagination was my comfort and delight. My fantasy world saved me as a child from my external environment, which was sometimes loving and comfortable, sometimes confusing and harsh.

I was a teenager in the 50's. Like many teens of that era, I wore white buck shoes and pleated skirts, and I jitterbugged to the music of Elvis and Bill Haley's Comets. A major influence came into my life to turn my head away from all this. It was a teacher of English who introduced me to the great ones—Shakespeare, Plato, Aristotle, the English Romantic Poets. One line from a poem of Shelley had particularly impressed me:

Life is like a dome of many-colored glass;
The One remains; the many change and pass.

This resounded in me like a deep message from my primal roots. "The One remains...," it had said. And the rest of my life was devoted to finding the road to this "One."

At sixteen, my English teacher had been the catalyst for me to change my perception of life. So influenced was I, that later I became an English teacher too. All through college I had been intensely dedicated. I graduated Phi Beta Kappa with notions of getting my MA and PhD. But graduate school lasted one semester for me. I went to Berkeley's Graduate Department of English—full of tweed blazers and aromatic pipes, scholars and critics. I didn't fit in; I loved the mystical poets like Blake and Emily Dickinson. I wrote one paper where I said, "With piercing mystical glares, they can see infinity finitely, crush the cosmos into a tangible ball, and live a million years past their allotted times." My teacher liked the paper enough, but she commented that closer inspection of diction and verse meters might be in order. What really interested me, however, was the eternal essence and metaphysical metaphors of the poems. Soon I left the ivy halls, and not long after, I moved back to Chicago and began to teach English in three different high schools for the next five years.

I loved teaching. I threw myself into it, grading papers until all hours of the night, writing paragraphs to the students on all their papers, holding lively discussions in class. I received a "Golden Apple Award" for one of the top ten teachers. But by my fifth year, the entire scenario had changed. I was in a school in the late 1960's where the students were rioting regularly. The school was in a uproar. My personal life was upside down, and sometimes I'd come home and stare at walls or sit between two speakers listening to music and stringing beads. I finally became a devotee of the great Aspirin. I even took Fiorinal, a drug I later found out contained barbiturates. I was smoking a lot, drinking a lot of coffee, and eating too many Hostess Ho Ho's.

In 1970 I moved back to California. I was frazzled, exhausted, looking for a way to soothe the tensions in my body and the malaise of my mind. Someone suggested I try a hatha yoga class. I was reluctant because I didn't know much about yoga, but I went. I went to the Integral Yoga Institute on Dolores Street in San Francisco. It smelled like clean food and incense, and I went upstairs to the yoga room. After the hatha yoga postures, we were led into a deep relaxation process. I was ecstatic! This was way beyond aspirin; this relaxed me more than anything I'd known. I knew this was going to be a panacea for my raw nerves and classical burnout case. I kept going, and I kept meditating. Ultimately meditation became more than a panacea for me. It became the center of my life. It relaxed me, that's for certain, but it also led me to a complete alteration of my perspective. It pointed me inward, and I realized that my difficulties had given me my greatest opportunities. My life was completely new. From that time on, I tried many forms of meditation, yoga, and growth, and I studied with spiritual teachers from all over the world.

During these years I also had great challenges. One of them came when my daughter and I were in a time of transition, and we needed to leave our home in Bolinas. We hadn't found any other place to live, so we set up tents for ourselves high on a hill by the ocean. At first it was an adventure. I saw it as a chance to learn how to find my own temple inside myself, to ease with change, to simplify my needs. But I wasn't the total trooper. It was beginning to rain, and we were getting moldy and wet. I felt myself going through so much intense change that even my handwriting was new. I looked to my highest self for guidance, but then I'd fall into a morass of fear and self-pity. One day at a fair, a wandering minstrel came over to me and whispered a haiku poem in my ear:

Since my house burned down,
Now I have a better view of the rising moon.

I laughed and laughed with the synchronicity of his poetry. I realized that sometimes I was able to see the moon, and other times I didn't even know it was there at all.

I understood that sometimes things must fall apart to be re-created and that everything is transitory. This was a perfect challenge for me to deal with my attachments, to learn how to bend and flow. I learned that the universe truly was caring for me, even though I had so many challenges all around, and I needed a dwelling place to call home. I realized that when I was able to travel deeply into the inner recesses of my pain, I learned many truths and ultimately could find myself coming out on the other side.

A palm reader looked at my hand and said, "You are coming out of a period of limitation and restriction. Spiritually and creatively you will have great manifestation." This fed my spirits, and before long I moved into a new period of my life.

In 1974, I met Baba Muktananda, a meditation teacher from India. At first, I was skeptical, but my skepticism melted after I received shaktipat, the transmission of spiritual meditation energy. Baba hit me over the head with a sheaf of peacock feathers, and I began to meditate deeply. I went so deeply into my own being that my mind stopped, became devoid of all thoughts. Finally thoughts returned, and my first one was, "Oh my God, this is real!" This meditation was the deepest I had known. I felt as if a blanket of peace had been thrown around me. My body began to shake involuntarily, doing spontaneous yogic breaths or pranayamas without my having willed them.

I began to see myself more clearly, see the layer of garbage that had been clogging my body and brain for so many years—pains in my body and emotions, my various addictions, especially to sugar. Step by step I began to unravel these through yoga, fasting, studying spiritual books, bodywork, holistic health, and especially inner processes like the ones you are reading about in this book. I did whatever I could do to cleanse and heal my body and mind. My meditation practice is still strong, though I no longer follow any one path.

In 1976, I began to offer individual consultations in inner healing and visualization and taught classes in San Francisco at Holistic Life University. I gave a number of workshops, and I also taught meditation and yoga in many other settings— corporations, universities, senior centers.

In the eighties, I was again dealing with economic issues that pushed every insecurity button I had, but ultimately I was able to find faith and trust. I studied transpersonal psychology in graduate school and became certified as a hypnotherapist.

My work as a hypnotherapist grows and thrives. I see my challenges all these years as great learning experiences for me. They taught me compassion; they taught me I could keep falling off my horse and get right back on and ride. In the early years, I wrote a poem about Sisyphus, the man of myth who kept pushing the boulder up the hill and watching it roll down, only to go back down and push it up, over and over:

> *Resilience—*
> > *to spring back up*
> > *like a rubber ball*
> > *Kept Sisyphus pushing*
> > *his boulder*
> > > *up that mountain*
> > *And is ultimately the quality*
> > *that belongs to those*
> > *who daily*
> *Save themselves.*

I have learned that everything has its perfect timing and that if you persevere and keep on watering your seeds, you will see your garden when the time is right for all its flowers to grow.

"And I have felt
A presence that disturbs me with the joy
Of elevated thoughts; a sense sublime
Of something far more deeply interfused,
Whose dwelling is the light of setting suns,
And the round ocean and the living air,
And the blue sky, and in the mind of man:
A motion and a spirit, that impels
All thinking things, all objects of all thought,
And rolls through all things."

Wordsworth

Recommended Reading

Here are some books on hypnosis that are worth reading. You can find many of them in bookstores, or you can write to a publishing company that specializes in hypnosis books for a catalog of titles. Write to:

Westwood Publishing Co.,
312 Riverdale Dr.
Glendale, CA 91204

I recommend any of Ormand McGill's informative and fascinating hypnosis books, some of which you can obtain from Westwood. Some of McGill's titles are: HYPNOTISM AND MYSTICISM OF INDIA, PROFESSIONAL STAGE HYPNOTISM, POWER HYPNOSIS HYPNOTHERAPY and many other superb books.

A classic, Dave Elman's book simply called HYPNOTHERAPY is a must for those interested in rapid inductions, hypnoanesthesia, and hypnotherapeutic techniques.

Gil Boyne, the director of the American Council of Hypnotist Examiners, has written a book that you can order from Westwood called TRANSFORMING THERAPY: A NEW APPROACH TO HYPNOTHERAPY.

HYPNOSIS QUESTIONS AND ANSWERS, by Zilbergeld, Edelstien, and Aroaz,is a collection of writings on hypnosis that covers a wide range of topics about what hypnosis is and how it works.

John G. Watkins has written HYPNOTHER-
APEUTIC TECHNIQUES, a comprehensive book
about the clinical applications of hypnosis.

There are many different approaches to
hypnotherapy, some of which can be found in books
on Neuro-Linguistic Programming, Alchemical
Hypnotherapy, Ericksonian Hypnotherapy, Medical
and Dental Hypnosis, Self-Hypnosis, and many other
orientations.

Some other helpful books are:

HOW TO HYPNOTIZE YOURSELF
   AND OTHERS, Rachel Copelan
HYPNOSIS FOR CHANGE, Josie Hadley
SELECTIVE AWARENESS, Peter Mutke, M.D.
SELF-HYPNOSIS IN TWO DAYS, Freda Morris
ALCHEMICAL HYPNOTHERAPY, David Quigley
MIND POWER, Bernie Zilbergeld, Ph.D. and
   Arnold Lazarus, Ph.D.

Quotation Sources

THE HEALING OF EMOTION, Chris Griscom, Simon & Schuster Inc., New York, 1988

ESSENCE: THE DIAMOND APPROACH TO INNER REALIZATION, A.H.Almaas, Samuel Weiser, York Beach, ME 1986

A GRADUAL AWAKENING, Stephen Levine, Anchor Press/ Doubleday, Garden City, NY 1979

THE BOOK OF RUNES, Ralph Blum, St. Martin's Press, NY 1982

WHERE ARE YOU GOING?, Swami Muktananda, Gurudev Siddha Peeth, Ganeshpuri, India 1981

THE ESSENTIAL WORDSWORTH, ed. Seamus Heaney, The Ecco Press, New York 1988

THE BOOK OF MIRDAD, Mikhail Naimy, Penguin Books, Baltimore, 1962

"Wind Bell", "The Five Skandas" by Abbot Tenshin Reb Anderson, Zen Center, Volume XXII, Fall 1988

SamuEl: Inner Guide

Further Information and Workshops

If you're interested in any of the hypnotherapy programs (including individual sessions, workshops, and cassette tapes), if you'd like to set up a hypnotherapy workshop in your area, or if you'd like a free brochure please contact me. For ordering books or tapes, please see order form page.

I'd love to hear from you to find out how the techniques are helping you and any other comments you'd like to make.

Marilyn Gordon
PO Box 10795
Oakland, CA 94610

(415) 547-8823

Audio Cassette Tapes

WonderWords™ tapes are carefully designed to give you the experience of renewal, inspiration, and healing. They are not your ordinary run-of-the-mill hypnosis tapes. Marilyn Gordon's clear and soothing voice accompanied by Grady Harris' original piano and synthesizer music bring you into a state of elevation and peace, enabling your mind and body to touch your essence. Some of the tapes create practical results, such as stopping smoking, losing weight, and sleeping well; others bring forth experiences of inner wisdom and higher consciousness. The newest tape is "Experiencing Your Essence".

EXPERIENCING YOUR ESSENCE
Get in touch with your source with the help of this beautiful tape.
Inspiring music by Irene Sazer.

SELF-HYPNOSIS
Learn this miraculous self-hypnosis technique to improve the quality
of your life. (This tape comes without music.)

THE EXPERIENCE OF LOVE
Open to the healing force of love. Love your inner child and find your
own higher power. Great for people in recovery.

VISUALIZATION HEALING
Enter six doorways leading to profound healing experiences.
Stimulate your immune system; heal body and mind.

EASY WEIGHT LOSS
Change the way you think about food; learn a method for training yourself to
eat more wisely so your body will shed unwanted pounds safely.

NO MORE SMOKING
Respect your body, change your habits, and give up smoking forever.
Learn techniques for successfully conquering tobacco addiction.

JOURNEY TO SELF-KNOWLEDGE
A guided journey to your inner wisdom. Learn how to make your dreams
come true, change habits, experience peace of mind.

GET A GOOD NIGHT'S SLEEP
Float into deep, restful sleep, and awaken in the morning rejuvenated.
Overcome insomnia with self-hypnosis.

TEN MINUTE STRESS MANAGER
Relax in the midst of busy day – or anytime when you want
to let go of stress rapidly.

Book Order Form

Please send _____ copy(ies) of HEALING IS REMEMBERING WHO
YOU ARE to:

Name_____

Address_____

City_____State_____Zip_____

Enclose $9.95 per book (See mailing address below). Sales Tax: Please add 7.25% sales tax for
books shipped to California addresses. Shipping: Book rate: $1.25 for the first book and 75 cents for
each additional book. UPS: $2.50 per book. Surface shipping may take 3-4 weeks. Please make
checks payable to WiseWord Publishing.

Cassette Order Form

Please mail the indicated tapes to:

Name_____

Address_____

City_____State_____Zip_____

ITEM	QTY.	PRICE
M100 EXPERIENCING YOUR ESSENCE ($9.95 ea.)		
M101 SELF-HYPNOSIS ($9.95 ea.)		
M102 THE EXPERIENCE OF LOVE ($9.95 ea.)		
M103 VISUALIZATION HEALING ($9.95 ea.)		
M104 EASY WEIGHT LOSS ($9.95 ea.)		
M105 NO MORE SMOKING ($9.95 ea.)		
M106 JOURNEY TO SELF-KNOWLEDGE ($9.95 ea.)		
M107 GET A GOOD NIGHT'S SLEEP ($9.95 ea.)		
M108 TEN MINUTE STRESS MANAGER ($9.95 ea.)		

Enclose $9.95 per tape (See mailing address below). Sales Tax: Please add 7.25% sales tax for tapes
shipped to California addresses. Shipping: Tape rate: $1.25 for the first tape and 75 cents for each
additional tape. UPS: $2.50 per tape. Surface shipping may take 3-4 weeks. Please make checks
payable to WiseWord Publishing.

Mail to:

Or for further information:
Marilyn Gordon/WiseWord Publishing
P.O. Box 10795 • Oakland, CA 94610
(415) 547-8823